CW01512705

THE PAI
WRITERS
BOOK OF

GAGS AND
ROUTINES

Bob Heather and Cheryl Barrett

From gags to riches - how to transform your
pantomime script

The Pantomime Writers book of Gags and Routines

Bob Heather & Cheryl Barrett

Published by Dublar
First published in Great Britain 2014
© Bob Heather and Cheryl Barrett 2014

All rights reserved.
No part of this publication may be reproduced in any form or by any means without the written permission of the publishers

ISBN 978-1-902659-07-7

Front cover photo:- Leighton Fort and Malcolm Clarke in 'Robin Hood' by Bob Heather and Cheryl Barrett at the Plaza Theatre, Romsey

Photograph by Matthew Ellison

This book is dedicated to the memory of
pantomime writer, director and grand dame
Chris Harris

1942 - 2014

Foreword

Christopher Biggins

Pantomime is an unusual animal, a completely different genre to any other form of theatre, but it always holds such a strong fascination for me. Having written, directed, produced and starred in over fifty productions, I know what a joy panto can bring to people – I still relish  every boo, hiss, cheer and chuckle. I performed my first pantomime in the seventies and was in for quite a shock - I found that nothing was as straightforward as it seemed. There were whole sections just marked 'routine', what was that all about? The old pantomime stalwarts and comics weren't fazed as they knew exactly what to do, but to me, everything seemed so alien.

Today, modern pantomime scripts have everything written in for the benefits of the cast and director, but if you are a pantomime script writer, how do you come up with ideas for these routines and what do you need to do to explain to director and cast what is required?

It so happens that Bob Heather and Cheryl Barrett have come to your aid with this wonderful collection of gags and routines, all updated, cleaned, and made politically correct (so many weren't in the heyday of vaudeville, variety, and pantomime), including some of which I must admit are new to me, which makes this little tome so modern and up to date.

Bob and Cheryl have been acting, directing, and writing pantomime scripts separately for some time, then after meeting up at an intensive pantomime workshop with Dougie Squires, they decided to pool resources and work together producing many wonderful scripts. Some of them are different stories to the norm, but all are absolutely traditional family entertainment.

Since they started working together, their scripts have become so loved and well-known they are performed all over the world as well as every corner of the UK. What they don't know about pantomime, you could write on the back of a theatre ticket stub. They also travel the length and breadth of the country with their well-received pantomime workshops.

To the aspiring pantomime script writer (and even the professional ones) this book is just what the doctor ordered. It not only lists dozens of gags and routines, but they all are explained and most of them scripted ready for you to put your own mark on the routine, and pop into your script. I only wish this book was around when I started writing panto scripts.

This wonderful little book covers everything from running gags to full routines, and also has a section of knock-knocks and jokes as well as a section on how to put visual comedy into any panto script. If you are a panto writer, or hope to start writing or directing, this book should be at the top of your shopping list – Oh yes it should...

Christopher Biggins as Mrs Smee in Peter Pan, Southend-on-Sea 2014.
Qdos Pantomimes.

LIST OF CONTENTS

LIST OF ILLUSTRATIONS

Photo credits

Fig 1, 2, and Front cover	Matthew Ellison
Fig 3, 11, 15	Clair Whitaker
Fig 4, 5, 8, 9	Bob Heather
Fig 10, 12	Plaza Archives

All illustrations and drawings by Bob Heather

INTRODUCTION

For many theatres, the pantomime season is a saviour. Drama, musicals, plays, and one-night shows cannot be relied upon to cover the running costs of the theatre, let alone make profits. The pantomime season, however, is the time of year when it can often be relied upon to bring in some much-needed cash to help societies and drama groups ease their way through the following year. In many cases a pantomime also does an excellent job of bringing the local community together.

What is that special formula that brings excited audiences into the theatre? It is the humour - everyone goes for a good laugh no matter what their age; from six to a hundred and six, people enjoy a good pantomime. So if you are writing a pantomime script, remember to use your jokes on two levels at all times - jokes for children and humour for adults. Make sure all your jokes for the mums and dads go straight over the children's heads. Another sure-fire way of using tried and tested humour in your script in order to please everyone from children to grandparents, is the use of pantomime gags and routines.

So what is a gag or routine? To most people it is synonymous with a joke, but there is a vast difference. A joke is humour passed on by word of mouth, but a gag or routine is invariably acted out.

Before we look at the different styles of gags (or running gag to give them their correct title) and routines, let us remind ourselves of the conventions and traits of pantomime. All good Fairies must only enter and exit down-stage right (from the actor's viewpoint) and must never cross the centre stage area. Likewise an immortal Villain (Wicked Fairy, Wizard, ogre, Demon, etc.) must only enter and exit down-stage left and never cross the centre line - that way we define good and evil. Mortal Villains and Baddies such as the Sheriff of Nottingham and the Wicked Squire must still only enter and exit stage left, but they are able to use the whole stage area.

Let's start with the running gags.

A running gag is a gag that keeps cropping up at different times throughout the pantomime performance.

The very first running gag that most audience members and actors come across is usually the Comic's introduction or "Hiya Gang". This is closely followed with the "Teddy Bear Gag", "The Flower Gag" or something similar. You will find all these in detail in our "Running Gags" section in this book.

In our pantomime *'Robin Hood'*, the running gag we devised was the Archers Theme being played whenever anyone mentioned the archers - after which everyone on-stage yelled out "Be quiet" or "Shut that row", to which the music stopped abruptly with a nasty scratching sound as though somebody had quickly taken the needle off a record.

Now let's look at the routines.

This is where this book comes into its own. Routines are mini sketches that don't necessarily have any bearing on the panto story. They are written to fill out, lengthen, or even occupy the whole of a front-of-cloth scene to give the stage crew time to change the set behind the cloth – although routines can also be used in full stage scenes as well.

Most scripts nowadays have the routine fully written within its pages, although it wasn't that long ago, professional pantomime scripts would start a new scene by just saying "Pheasant routine", or "Ghost routine", and sometimes would only say "Business" or "Routine", where the comic would insert his own take on his favourite routine.

Routines can vary in length from a few lines to a whole scene. If you decide to place any of these routines into your scripts, make sure that you re-write them and give them your own personal slant - not just copy them down wholesale. If you are anything of a reasonable pantomime writer, these routines will be a breeze to re-write, and you can base the circumstances on the location and story-line of your own particular script.

Just remember not to overdo your routines – always leave the audience wanting more. To get the idea of how these routines work, it is always worth checking YouTube to see how they appear to the audience. Just type in "pantomime routine" and you'll be surprised at how many there are.

It is getting more and more difficult to find the routines written down nowadays, so that is why we have introduced this book. We hope you will find it invaluable as your pantomime script-writing career unfolds ahead of you.

Please feel free to use the gags and routines from this book in your scripts, but make sure you re-write them first. Try to make them feel fresh and fit in with the theme of your panto.

Visual gags.

Before we look at the running gag and routine listings, let us look at visual gags. Visual gags are exactly what it says on the tin. These aren't always put in the scripts by the writers, although sometimes they might feel the need to write a visual into the script the way they see it. Visual gags are usually placed into a performance by the director. A good director often spots ideal places within the script to add visual gags. For instance, you might have a scene in the panto where the chorus are on stage in a song and dance number. It could be in the market place or a village square, but you have decided that a Morris dance would be ideal for this scene. In order to add a bit of visual humour into it, the Dame, or another Character comes on-stage just after the dance has started, miming away to the music on an accordion.

Sometimes a visual gag can be so easy to use, but can alter the scene for the better. For instance, in the school-room scene, you can drive a small nail into the blackboard. This can't be seen by the Audience, but when the Comic goes to hang up his jacket, he takes the chalk and draws a coat-hook on the blackboard around the nail. He then hangs his coat on the nail, looking as though he has hung it on the hook that he has just drawn.

If there's a palace scene, a cuckoo clock can be hung on the wall. The cuckoo can be operated by a stage-hand with his arm in a black sleeve. It can pop out, say "Cuckoo" and pop back again. It can even grab people, or things off passing trays etc.

You might also have a scene where several characters are sat down such as in the school-scene - on a given point in the script, all the characters cross their legs simultaneously, then later, cross them back again. It is little things like this that can make all the difference to humour in a pantomime. These little ideas are simple to put into practice and they will always get you extra laughs and Brownie points. There was one of our pantomimes where the King fell off the stage losing his crown and wig. The Audience thought it was extremely funny. People afterwards were saying "We were there the night the King fell off the stage". Little did they know he did it every performance.

When Bob directed our pantomime *'Robin Hood'*, the comic, Wally Scarlet had to make himself scarce because the Sheriff's henchmen were approaching. Instead of leaving the stage, Bob got Wally to reach into the wings and grab a painted

canvas outfit, which he quickly dropped over his head and was immediately disguised as a tree trunk complete with knot-hole which he spied through. To add to this gag, when the Sheriff came on stage to speak to his henchmen, Wally used an owl hand puppet to appear in the knot-hole. The owl followed the conversation by moving his wings and turning his head to look at whoever was talking.

Fig 1 – *Leighton Fort as the Sheriff of Nottingham, with the Tree-trunk disguise and the owl puppet (inset).*

~~~(*D*)~~~

Fig 2 – Cheryl Barrett as Holly Jockey Sticks (The Local Woodland Fairy) from 'Robin Hood' by Bob Heather and Cheryl Barrett.

RUNNING GAGS

Let us start with a few running gags. These are silly gags that the Comic or Dame repeats on nearly every entrance they make, cumulating, sometimes, in a tag which he/she does on his/her last entrance. The first gag in this book is the most common gag to be found in almost every pantomime script ever written.

Hiya Gang

On the Comic's first entrance, he should introduce himself to the Audience; he then tells the children that every time he comes on and shouts, "Hiya kids", they must shout back "Hiya Billy", or whatever his name is. He then gets the Audience to try it out. After the first try, he tells them they weren't very loud and asks them to do it again. He goes through this two or three more times. By the last time he tries the call-out, the Audience will be hopefully shouting back at a deafening volume. After that, every time the Comic comes on stage he'll do the call-out and get a resounding reply. The call-out and answer can be almost anything from "Watcha mates", where the Audience respond with "Watcha Billy", or "Hi de ho", when they answer after the Comic has called out "Hi de hi". The Comic could even put his right hand up in the air and shout "Give me five", and the Audience respond by putting their right hands up and shouting back "Yo". You can even create your own greeting, such as "Is everybody happy?" with the answer, "You bet your boots we are". The ideas are endless.

This could also be done with characters like the Comic Duo. Every time they come on stage, the first one enters and calls out "Where are you" in a sing-song style, to which the other one comes on calling "I'm coming" in exactly the same sing-song style. If this happens every time they make an entrance, you will probably find that before long, the Audience will all be joining in with the answering call, in the same sing-song style.

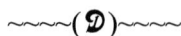

The Little Flower

In this gag, upon the Comic's first entrance, he is carrying a flower in a pot or bucket. Throughout the performance, the flower grows taller and taller as if by magic. The kids think this is wonderful.

Comic: Oh hello everyone, I didn't see you there. What do you think of my little flower eh? It's a rambling Daisy. Here – I'll let you all into a little secret. I'm useless at gardening and I keep forgetting to water it. **(He gets an idea.)** Hey, I say - I've just had a little thought. Whenever I come on, can you to remind me to water it? Will you do that?

(Audience reaction.)

Comic: I can't hear you – you'll have to shout louder than that. I said can you remind me to water it?

(Audience reaction.)

Comic: Oh goody – I'll just put it down here then. **(He puts it down in a pre-determined position next to the pros arch.)** Shall we give it a little go – Are you ready?

(Audience reaction.)

Comic: You need to be louder than that. Don't forget, whenever I come on I want you all to shout "Water your little flower". Right, I'll go off and come back on again.

(Comic exits, then re-enters. There is a reaction from the Audience.)

Comic: That wasn't very good was it? You need to be much louder - let's try it again.

(Once more the Comic exits then re-enters.)

Audience: Water your little flower.

Comic: That was a bit better, but still not loud enough. Let's try it one more time.

(Again the Comic exits then re-enters.)

Audience: Water your little flower.

Comic: That was brilliant. Now I can get on and water my little flower. **(He looks all around.)** Oh dear. I seem to have forgotten my watering can; I'll just go and get it – don't go away.

(The Comic exits, then re-enters with his watering can carrying it carefully as though it is full of water, but when he gets near the front of the stage, he stumbles and does a little trip causing the Audience to think he is going to spill water all over them. Audience reaction.)

Comic: Whoops. **(He waters the flower then puts his watering can next to it.)**

Comic: That's better. Well I must go now, don't forget to remind me to water my little flower whenever I come on. Bye now. **(He exits, waving to the audience.)**

After that, every time the Comic comes on stage, the Audience shouts, and he will water the flower. To everyone's astonishment it grows and grows until by the end of the show it is very tall. This is achieved by the Comic fixing a piece of fishing line on to the plant when he first places it. The line runs over the scenery and down the other side where a stage-hand pulls the line every time the plant is watered. The plant must have a long stem coiled in the bottom of the pot or bucket with a weight on the end of it for the gag to work.

The Hanky Gag

This running gag involves several handkerchiefs of various sizes. When the Comic enters for the first time, he sniffs a few times and the Dame says, "Where's your hanky?" He takes a small hanky out of his pocket and loudly blows his nose. The Dame then tells the Audience that if the Comic sniffs again, they must shout out "Where's your hanky?" From now on, whenever the Comic is on stage and sniffs, the Audience will shout out to him "Where's your hanky?" Each time they shout and he pulls out his hanky to blow his nose, the hanky gets bigger. The last time he does this, usually in the finale; the handkerchief is very large. As an alternative, he can pull out a lot of different coloured hankies tied together just like a magician does with flags. This will always get a good laugh.

The Teddy Bear

This is usually used at the Comic's first entrance, where he introduces the children to his Teddy, Rabbit, Dog, Snail, or whatever, he then puts it in the corner of the stage by the pros arch where everyone can see it. He asks the Audience if they can look after it for him and that if anyone goes near, or touches his Teddy during the show, they must call him. During the course of the show, several different characters will try to take the Teddy, and when the children call the Comic, he dutifully runs on shouting "Who's touching my Teddy?" This is a very clever contrivance for getting the Comic to appear on stage at any time, especially if there is no logic or reason for him to do so – just get any character to go near the Teddy and the Audience will call the Comic on. At the walk-down and bows at the end of the show, the Comic will walk down, pick up his Teddy and do his bow.

Fig 3 - *Leigh Normington as Billy Goose with his pet Snail from 'Mother Goose' by Bob Heather and Roger Lamb.*

Don't Pull The Lever

For this gag you need a large lever or bell-push fixed to the pros arch with a notice under it saying, 'Don't pull the lever' or 'Don't push the button'. During the Comic's first entrance he tells the Audience that if they see anyone approach the lever or button, they are to shout out "Don't pull the lever" ("Don't push the button"). From then on, whenever any character goes to pull the lever, the Audience will shout out and the character that is about to do the dastardly deed quickly leaves the lever alone and moves away. At the end of the show the Comic explains that he doesn't know what the lever (button) does and he is going to pull it to find out. The children will shout for him not to, but he pulls it regardless amid yells of "Don't pull the lever", setting off a pyro that covers the stage and the first half dozen rows of the auditorium with cascades of shimmering metallic confetti.

For something slightly different, when the Comic pulls the lever, there could be a loud whirring sound effect and a large hammer or club made of foam rubber, handled by a stage hand hidden in the wings, hits the Comic on the head, knocking him over.

This can also be done with a contrivance that looks like a communication cord from a train, with the notice "Don't pull the chain", or "For emergency only".

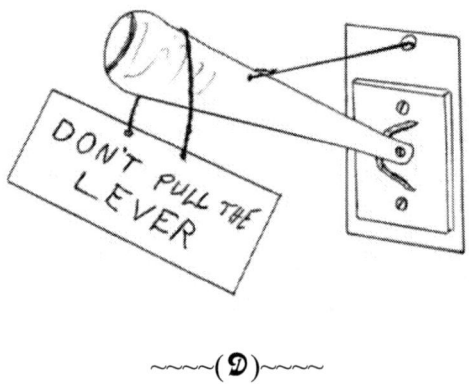

~~~~(𝔇)~~~~

ROUTINES

This is the section of the book you have all been waiting for isn't it?

Oh no it's not!

Oh yes it is!

Many routines over the years have involved money changing hands – but not all. Sometimes it is the Dame getting the better over the Squire when handing over her rent, sometimes it is different characters trying to get the better over each other by betting a fiver or more that they can do this, see that, or hear something else, with hilarious consequences.

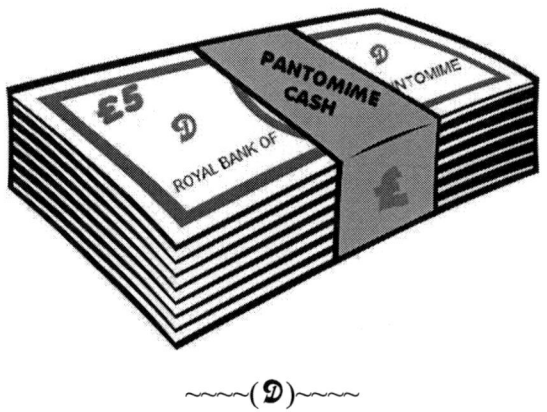

~~~~($\mathcal{D}$)~~~~

Payback Routine

This gag can be used whenever the Dame is paying back the rent to the Squire or landlord. Although with tweaking it can be re-worded to suit most pantomime situations.

(Everyone is stood around the market square. The Squire demands that the Dame pays him the rent that she owes.)
Squire: Where's the ten weeks rent you owe me?

Dame: It so happens that I won a little money on the lottery today so you are in luck. Now, how much do I owe you?

Squire: You owe me fifty pounds for that hovel, er – I mean cottage.

Dame: Fifty pounds?

Squire: Fifty pounds – and I want it now.

Dame: Ok Squire, hold out your hand. **(She starts counting the money into his hand.)** One, two, three, four – er, how many weeks did you say I owed?

Squire: Ten weeks.

Dame: Ten weeks?

Squire: Yes, ten.

Dame: **(Carries on counting the money.)** Eleven, twelve, thirteen, fourteen – how many other people in the village owe you rent Squire?

Squire: Twenty two.

Dame: **(Carries on counting the money.)** Twenty three, Twenty four – That must be an awful lot of rent they owe you.

Squire: Yes, when you've paid me I will still be owed sixty-five pounds.

Dame: Sixty-five?

Squire: Yes, sixty-five.

Dame: **(She goes to carry on paying.)** Sixty si... Here, hang on a minute, I only owe you fifty pounds.

Squire: That's right.

Dame: I've just paid you sixty five. Give me back my money - I have overpaid you by fifteen pounds.

Squire: **(Flustered.)** What? Oh yes. **(He counts the money back into the Dames hand.)** One, two, three, four, five, six, seven, eight, nine, ten... **(He looks at his now empty hand in bewilderment.)**

Dame: Hang on a minute – you owed me fifteen pounds but you only paid back ten. You still owe me another fiver.

Squire: I'm sorry - I don't know how that happened. **(He takes a fiver out of his pocket and gives it to her.)**

Dame: Thank you very much Squire. Now we're all square. **(She hurriedly exits.)**

Squire: Hang on a minute, I've been diddled. **(He chases off after her.)** Come back here this minute you old harridan.

Fig 4 - *David Tatnall as Cap'n Slog, and Colin Russell as Sarah the cook, from 'Dick Whittington' by Bob Heather.*

It's Behind You

This was always called the ghost routine in the past because of a ghost creeping up behind the cast, but it doesn't have to be a ghost, it can be used with anything depending on the pantomime. In the past, this routine has been used with a Ghost, an Egyptian Mummy, a Gorilla, a Demon - in fact almost anything can be creeping up on our gang of heroes.

(At the start of the gag there are four people on stage, Sarah the Dame, Billy, Dopey and Dippy.)

Billy: I don't like the look of this place.

Dopey: It feels ever so creepy.

Dippy: I bet it's haunted.

Billy: I want to go.

Sarah: You should have gone before you came out.

Billy: I mean I want to go home.

Dopey: I hope there aren't any ghosts round here.

Billy: Well if a ghost does appear perhaps all the boys and girls will shout out and warn us.

Sarah: Will you do that boys and girls? If you see a ghost or anything, shout out loud so we'll know. Will you do that for us?

(Audience reaction.)

Sarah: You're going to have to be louder than that. Will you do that for us?

(Audience reaction.)

Sarah: That's better – I feel much safer now.

Dippy: Well I still feel scared.

Sarah: Oh you big girls blouse, there's nothing to worry about. I've heard that the best way of keeping away ghosts, is to sing a song.

Billy: Your singing would keep anything away.

Sarah: Watch it you.

Dopey: What shall we sing?

Billy: I know, let's sing Teddy Bear's Picnic.

(They all start to sing. The Ghost enters and walks straight across the stage behind them and off the other side. The Audience shout.)

Billy: **(To Audience.)** Did you say something?

All: **(Together.)** What - a ghost? Where?

(More Audience reaction.)

All: Over there? **(Pointing.)** We'd better go and have a look then.

(They walk round to look for the Ghost who has now gone.)

Sarah: There's nothing there.

All: **(Together, swinging their arms in unison, in time with the chant.)** We'd better sing it again then, hadn't we?

(They start to sing again and the Ghost walks across the stage behind them, and off the other side again. Audience reaction.)

Billy: **(To Audience.)** Did you say something?

All: What - a ghost? Where?

(Audience reaction.)

Sarah: Where, over there? **(Pointing.)** We'd better go and have a look then.

(They walk around again but still don't see the Ghost.)

Sarah: There's nothing there.

All: **(Together, swinging their arms in unison, in time with the chant.)** We'd better sing it again then, hadn't we?

(They start to sing and this time the Ghost enters and stands behind Dippy. The Ghost taps him on the shoulder. Dippy turns and sees the Ghost, screams and is chased off by it. The rest carry on singing all through this, oblivious to the shouts of the Audience.)

Billy: **(To Audience.)** Did you say something?

Sarah: Where's Dippy?

(The Ghost re-appears behind them, and the Audience react.)

All: What - a ghost? Where - over there? **(Pointing.)**

(The Ghost disappears.)

All: We'd better go and have a look then.

(They all walk round together and find nothing.)

Sarah: There's nothing here.

All: **(Together, swinging their arms in unison, in time with the chant.)** We'd better sing it again then, hadn't we?

(They sing. Ghost enters; Dopy sees it, yells and runs off.)

Billy: **(To Audience.)** Did you say something?

Sarah: Where's Dopey?

(Audience reaction.)

All: What - a ghost? Where - over there? **(Pointing.)** We'd better go and have a look then.

(Once again they walk round and find nothing.)

Sarah: There's still nothing there.

Sarah: } **(Together, swinging their arms in unison, in time with the chant.)**

Billy: } We'd better sing it again then, hadn't we?

(They sing again. The Ghost enters and this time frightens Billy off.)

Sarah: Did you say something? **(She looks around.)** Where's Billy gone?

(Audience reaction.)

Sarah: Is that ghost still here?

(Audience reaction.)

Sarah: Where - over there? **(Pointing.)** I'd better go and have a look then. **(She walks around and finds nothing.)** I'd better sing it again then, all on my own.

(Sarah sings. The Ghost enters and stands next to her. The Audience shout and Sarah stops singing.)

Sarah: What - a ghost? Where - over there? **(Pointing.)** I'd better have a look then.

(Sarah slowly turns and sees the Ghost. The Ghost screams and runs off stage. Sarah shrugs her shoulders at the Audience, then exits. Black-out.)

All pantomimes should have at least one 'behind-you' moment. If you don't want to have a Ghost or Demon scene, then the 'behind-you' moment can be easily achieved in many different ways. Here is a different version of a "behind-you" routine.

Chorus 1: **(To Sarah.)** Isn't Billy with you?

Sarah: Isn't he here? I told him to meet me here in the market. Has anyone seen him?

(She looks out to Audience.)

Sarah: He's my son. You haven't seen him around have you? You'll recognise him when you see him; he's such a handsome lad.

Chorus 1: We'll help you look for him.

Chorus: **(All exit in different directions calling out.)** Billy. Billy.

Sarah: Oh dear I wonder where he's gone. If you see him you will let me know, won't you?

(Billy enters Up-Right and saunters down behind Sarah.)

Audience: He's behind you.

Sarah: He's where?

Audience: Behind you.

(Business – Sarah looks round behind her but Billy moves with her so he is behind her all the time. Sarah faces front again.)

Sarah: Oh no he isn't.

Audience: Oh yes he is.

Sarah: Oh no he isn't.

Audience: Oh yes he is.

Sarah: Well I can't see him… **(She turns and see's Billy and gives a little jump.)** Oh there you are Billy; you nearly gave me one of my conniptions. I've been looking everywhere for you. Where have you been?

~~~~($\mathcal{D}$)~~~~

Not Here Routine

There is nothing like a routine that treats people like they are absolute idiots. This routine is one of the best, and the kids love every minute of it.

Dame: **(To Salt.)** And where do you think you are going?

Salt: **(Jumps.)** Oh, I didn't see you there.

Dame: That's because I'm not here.

Salt: Yes you are, you're just there, look. **(He points.)**

Dame: That's not me. I'm just a delusion - a fig-roll of your imagination.

Salt: That's where you're wrong because I don't have any imagination.

Dame: **(Gives a wink to the Audience, and then turns back to Salt**.) I bet you five pounds I can prove I'm not here.

Salt: Go on then, prove it. Here's my fiver.

(They both put their money on the floor.)

Dame: Right. Now I'm not in Land's End am I?

Salt: No. Of course you're not in Land's End.

Dame: And I'm not in John O'Groats am I?

Salt: You're right; you're not in John O'Groats either.

Dame: And I'm not on the Isle of Wight?

Salt: You're certainly not on the Isle of Wight.

Dame: Well if I'm in none of these places, I must be somewhere else.

Salt: That's right.

Dame: Then if I'm somewhere else, I can't be here can I? I win. **(She picks up the money and exits laughing.)**

Salt: What a swindle. I'll have to try that on someone else to get my money back.

(Pepper enters.)

Pepper: Hello. What are you up to?

Salt: I'm not up to anything because I'm not here. **(He stamps his foot close to Pepper's.)**

Pepper: **(Jumping in pain.)** Of course you're here you've just stamped on my toe.

Salt: Well, I bet you ten pounds I can prove it wasn't me because I'm not here.

Pepper: Ten pounds?

Salt: Ten pounds.

Pepper: You're off your trolley. Go on then, go ahead and prove you're not here. Here's my tenner.

(They both put their money down.)

Salt:	Right. Now I'm not in Land's End am I?
Pepper:	No, you're not in Land's End.
Salt:	And I'm not in John O'Groats am I?
Pepper:	**(Scottish accent.)** Oh nay Jimmy, you're nay in John O'Groats.
Salt:	And I'm not on the Isle of Wight am I?
Pepper:	No, you need a boat to get to the Isle of Wight.
Salt:	Well if I'm in none of these places I must be somewhere else.
Pepper:	Yea you must be.
Salt:	And if I'm somewhere else I'm not here – I win.

(He picks up the money and exits.)

Pepper:	I think I've just been bamboozled out of my money. I'll have to try to get it back.

(Dame enters.)

Dame:	What are you doing stood standing here looking like a wet lettuce?
Pepper:	I was going to have some fun.
Dame:	Well you won't get much fun round here.
Pepper:	Oh I don't know, I think I'm just about to. Would you like to earn me some money? I mean would you like to *win* some money?
Dame:	**(Gives knowing wink to Audience.)** I wouldn't mind having a go. What do I do?
Pepper:	Well I bet you twenty pounds that I can prove that I'm not here.
Dame:	You don't have to prove you're not all there, everyone knows that already.
Pepper:	Bloomin' cheek!
Dame:	**(To Audience.)** Have you ever had a feeling that you've been somewhere before? **(To Pepper.)** Go on then, prove you're not here.

(They both put their money down.)

Pepper:	Right now, I'm not in the Land of Wight am I?
Dame:	No. you're not in the Land of Wight.
Pepper:	And I'm not on John's Isle am I?

Dame:	You are definitely not on John's Isle.
Pepper:	And I'm not in Groats End am I?
Dame:	You aren't in Groats End, no.
Pepper:	Well if I'm not in any of these places, I must be somewhere else.
Dame:	Well of course you must.
Pepper:	And if I'm somewhere else, I'm not here.
Dame:	You're right. **(She picks up all the money and starts to exit.)**
Pepper:	Hey that's my money. I've just won that.
Dame:	Don't be daft. How could that be your money? You're not here.

(Dame runs off chased by Pepper.)

Two Tens For A Five

We based this routine on part of the act used by Abbot and Costello extensively throughout their career. It is widely believed that the original idea came from the British variety acts they saw when they toured England just before the war.

(Simon and Billy are on stage. They are both holding a wad of money each. Billy's wad is much bigger than Simon's.)

Billy:	Isn't it wonderful now we've managed to earn some money. I hope the Squire doesn't realise we've been nicking his apples and selling them in the market.

(Simon looks at Billy's wad, then his own, then back to Billy's again. He looks puzzled.)

Simon:	It looks like you've got more money than me.
Billy:	No, it's just the way the light falls on it. But don't worry; I can now pay you back the fiver I owe you.
Simon:	Oh goody. **(Big smile.)**
Billy:	**(He takes a fiver from his wad and holds it towards Simon.)** Have you got two tens for a five?

Simon: (**Takes two tens from his wad.**) Certainly, here
you are.

(**Simon gives the two tens to Billy and takes the proffered
fiver and gives a big grin. Throughout Billy's next line,
Simon is looking at his wad and suddenly realises he has been
duped. He looks at Billy's wad, then his own.**)

Billy: Look at all this money. I think I'll go to *[local]*
restaurant for a slap up meal.

Simon: (**A bit angry.**) Hang on, hang on. Fifteen pounds
has just gone south.

Billy: What do you mean?

Simon: Fifteen much needed quids have just disappeared
into thin air.

Billy: What are you suggesting?

Simon: You and all your fancy talking – you've just
bamboozled me.

Billy: Are you accusing me of cheating?

Simon: Well, er… No… er yes - you took two tens for a
five.

Billy: Oh, I'm very sorry. (**Takes another fiver from
his wad.**) Here's your five back – now give me back my two
tens.

Simon: (**He gives Billy the two tens and takes the
fiver.**) That's better. (**He looks pleased with himself.**)

(**Throughout Billy's next line, Simon looks at his wad and
suddenly realises he has been duped again, looking from one
wad to the other.**)

Billy: I think I might even have enough to go on a nice
holiday in the sunshine. Now where shall I go?

Simon: (**To Audience.**) Hang on a minute - he's done it
again. But don't worry; I have a plan to get my own back.

(**Simon taps Billy on the shoulder.**)

Simon: Now it's my turn, clever clogs. I'm getting fed
up being diddled by you. (**He takes two tens and offers
them to Billy.**) Here's your two tens, now give me back my
fiver.

(Billy gives Simon a fiver and takes the two tens.)

Simon: **(He give a big grin and runs off stage, shouting.)** That'll teach you to double-cross me. **(He exits.)**

Billy: What an idiot. **(He exits the opposite side.)**

(Simon enters again waving his wad of cash angrily having realised he's been duped yet again.)

Simon: Hey you – come back here. You've diddled me again. **(He chases off after Billy.)**

~~~~($\mathcal{D}$)~~~~

Interruption Routines

This type of routine has been around the vaudeville halls and variety theatres for years. When used in pantomime, it usually takes place in front-of-cloth scenes. It is either during a song (usually the Dame or Comic's song) when various cast and chorus members run on throughout the song and interrupt with a joke or stupid question to the point where the Dame or Comic gives up and leaves the stage. It can also work when two characters are talking idle chit-chat about what has happened, or something that furthers the story. The interruption idea can also be used to good effect with characters or chorus coming on and interrupting during a main scene to give added humour. Below is a small snippet of a different interruption routine to show how it can work. This is taken from *'Dick Whittington'* by Cheryl Barrett, when the French Sea Captain, Rock Eel is trying to 'chat up' Dame Sherry Trifle. Please do not use the actual piece below as it is copyright to Cheryl Barrett © 2011. The idea is to show how the routine works so you can write your version in your very own style. (See also "Knock Knock gags in the joke section on page 90, as they can also be used as interruption gags.)

Rock: **(He spots Sherry.)** Oh, Mais oui.

Sherry: **(To Audience.)** Ooh 'ain't he bold? **(To Rock.)** Of course we may.

(An Athlete runs across the stage with an Olympic torch giving Sherry a little wave as he passes.)

Rock: Oo eez zat?

Sherry: He's just an old flame.

Rock: I want to know more about you, what is your name? I am intrigued.

Sherry: I am Sherry Trifle.

Rock: Sherry Trifle - I wondered why you looked like a giant sundae. So what eez your father's name?

Sherry: 'Ere what's with all the questions? You're not from the social are you?

Rock: I am just eenterested. My father was an old sea dog, ee seldom came 'ome.

Sherry: My father was a dirty dog, he always came home. That's why there's so many of us. **(Plucks a strawberry from her hat.)** Can I tempt you to a strawberry?

Rock: **(Looks at her hat.)** Haven't you got a cherry?

Sherry: **(Knowing look to Audience.)** Oh, I lost that years ago.

Rock: **(Laughs.)** Ahhh, sweet Sherry... **(He pinches her cheeks.)** Or are you fortified?

Sherry: **(She whacks him.)** Forty five? - Bloomin' cheek. I haven't even touched thirty yet.

(Another old Athlete runs across stage with an Olympic torch and waves to Sherry.)

Rock: Oo eez that? Anuzzer old flame?

Sherry: **(Blows the Athlete a kiss.)** Yes, bless him. He still carries a torch for me.

~~~(**D**)~~~

Rice Pudding

This routine has been around since the early days of vaudeville and has been known as "Sticks", "Sweaty Socks", and even "Chips" in the past, which proves that you can use almost anything as the answer. It is another of the much-loved betting gags that seems to pop up quite often, and can be altered to suit any pantomime. When it was used in Bob's version of *'The Pied Piper'*, the word was changed to 'rats' to blend in with the rest of the panto script.

Billy: (**To Simon.**) I bet you a fiver you can't answer everything I say with the same word.
Simon: What do you mean - answer everything you say with the same word?
Billy: Whatever question I ask you, you must answer rice pudding.
Simon: Rice pudding - that's a daft answer, isn't it?
Billy: That's what you've got to say if you want to win.
Simon: I see. So if I say rice pudding to everything you ask; I'll win a fiver?
Billy: That's right. Now put your money down.
(Billy and Simon both put a five pound note on the floor.)
Billy: Now are you ready?
Simon: Yes, I'm ready.
Billy: (**Picking up the fivers.**) That's a fiver I've won.
Simon: What do you mean?
Billy: You didn't say rice pudding.
Simon: That's not fair. I didn't realize we'd started. I want another go?
Billy: Go on then, put down another fiver.
(Billy and Simon both put down another fiver each.)
Billy: Now, are you ready this time?
Simon: Rice pudding.
Billy: I didn't get you that time did I?
Simon: No you didn't – I'm not stupid.

Billy:	I'm saying nothing. **(He picks up the money.)**
Simon:	What are you doing?
Billy:	You didn't say rice pudding.
Simon:	Oh no, I've done it again. Let's have another go.

(Billy and Simon both put their money down.)

Billy:	Are you ready?
Simon:	Rice pudding.
Billy:	I didn't get you that time did I?
Simon:	Rice pudding.
Billy:	You're getting very good at this aren't you?
Simon:	Rice pudding.
Billy:	What's your dog's name?
Simon:	Fido.
Billy:	You lose again **(He picks up the money.)** You're supposed to say rice pudding.
Simon:	But his name is Fido, not rice pudding.
Billy:	Sometimes I wonder about you, I'll let you have another go.

(They both put their money down.)

Billy:	Are you ready?
Simon:	Rice pudding.
Billy:	I didn't get you that time did I?
Simon:	Rice pudding.
Billy:	What did you have for breakfast this morning?
Simon:	Rice pudding.
Billy:	What a strange thing to have for breakfast - what would you rather have, rice pudding or the money.
Simon:	The money.
Billy:	**(Picks up the money.)** You lose; you're supposed to say rice pudding.
Simon:	Oh no. Let's have one more go.
Billy:	This is your last chance.

(Billy and Simon both put their money down.)

Billy:	Are you ready?
Simon:	Rice pudding.
Billy:	I didn't catch you out that time did I?

Simon:	Rice pudding.
Billy:	You're getting very good at this aren't you?
Simon:	Rice pudding.
Billy:	Now listen carefully - what would you rather have - the rice pudding or the money?
Simon:	Rice pudding
Billy:	Right then, you have the rice pudding, and I'll have the money. **(He picks up the money and exits.)**
Simon:	Hey, you rotter - come back here with my hard earned money. **(He chases off after Billy.)**

~~~~(𝒟)~~~~

Decorating The Parlour

This is a very funny routine even if the audience may have seen it before at other pantomimes, variety shows, or even on TV. It is one of those routines that don't seem to get used so much nowadays because of the cost of slosh itself and the time involved in preparing and cleaning it up afterwards - as well as the expense of laundering two costumes after every performance. Remember that if you add this routine into your script, some drama societies may refuse to use it because of budget restrictions. However, there is room for change and addition to the routine depending on the length of time you want it to run. It is most advisable to make this routine the very last item before the interval in your script so that the stage crew have plenty of time to clean up afterwards. You can also use this idea to base many other versions of the routine, such as cleaning high shelves in a kitchen scene, window cleaning, or polishing mirrors as we did with our version of '*Snow White and the Seven Dwarfs*'.

(For this routine the props needed are as follows: a large paste table and a pair of steps are set upstage. On the table is a large paste brush and underneath it are a bucket of paste and two rolled pieces of wallpaper, each about two metres in length. The rest of the props can be placed anywhere convenient. After a couple of rehearsals you will know the best place to set the props to suit your action. Apart from the bucket of paste set under the table you will need three more buckets full of paste and three buckets of paint, an empty bucket without a bottom and a bucket with a hole in the side small enough to block with your finger. Use the usual slosh (or splosh) made of shaving soap for the wallpaper paste, or the slosh paste you can now get from Theatrical scenic stores. You will also need a thinner version of the slosh coloured with food colouring for the paint. Grabbit and Runn enter. Runn is wearing a bowler hat.)

Grabbit: (**Looking around in awe.**) Fancy the King and Queen asking us to do the decorating here.

Runn: (**Also looking around in awe.**) Do you know, this is the first time I have ever been inside the palace.

Grabbit: If we do a good job, we may be made knights.

Runn: Oh no, I much prefer the day shift

Grabbit: Idiot. This room looks as though it hasn't been decorated for years.

Runn: Don't worry about it, with my help; we'll have it done in a trice.

Grabbit: I'm always worried about your help - we mustn't make a mess or there'll be trouble.

Runn: Stop worrying, there won't be any mess. Where shall we start?

Grabbit: Just hold this bucket and I'll pour the paint in.

(**Grabbit gives Runn the bottomless bucket to hold. When he pours the paint in it goes all over Runn's shoes.**)

Runn: Euck, you've poured paint all over my shoes.

Grabbit: Oh I'm so sorry - I'd better use this other bucket.

(Grabbit fills the bucket with the hole in the side near the bottom with paint; he puts his finger over the hole so the paint doesn't leak out. He climbs a step ladder while Runn stands at the foot of the steps. Runn takes his hat off and holds it out while he ad-libs about the palace. Grabbit takes his finger away from the hole in the bucket, and the paint pours into Runn's hat. He puts his hat on and gets a soaking.)

Runn: What have you done? I'm overcome with emulsion.

Grabbit: Never mind, the colour goes with your eyes.

Runn: It's not fair. **(He shakes his arms.)**

Grabbit: Be careful. We mustn't make a mess. **(He comes down the steps.)** Pass me that bucket of paint there.

(Runn hands Grabbit a bucket of paint which Grabbit cradles in him arms.)

Grabbit: Now, get that paste ready and hold on to these steps.

(Runn places a bucket of paste at the bottom of the steps. He holds on to the steps and as Grabbit climbs them, the paint splashes out of the bucket he is cradling. It splashes all over Runn at the bottom of the steps.)

Grabbit: You're getting in a right mess down there. Why can't you be a bit more careful? **(He climbs back down the steps and puts his foot in the bucket of paste. The bucket gets stuck on his foot.)** Don't just stand there staring, help me get this off my foot.

(Runn pulls the bucket off Grabbit's foot and they both fall over.)

Runn: I think we should do the papering first. It's not as messy as painting.

Grabbit: That's the best idea you've had today. You can paste the paper.

(Runn puts the paper on the table and goes to paste it but every time he stops to get paste on the brush, the paper rolls up. After a few attempts at this he lifts his leg on to the table and holds the paper down with his foot while he pastes it.)

Grabbit: What do you think you're playing at? You're pasting the wrong side of the paper. You should paste the other side.

(Runn immediately starts to paste the underside of the table.)

Runn: Is that better?

Grabbit: No it isn't. Now take this paper and stick it on the wall.

(Runn picks up the pasted paper, climbs the steps with it unrolled in front of him so that as he climbs the steps he treads on the paper which tears off with every step. By the time he gets to the top of the steps he is left with a tiny piece of paper which he sticks on the wall. He looks at it, shakes his head, then peels it off, realigns it and sticks it back on the wall.)

Runn: How does that look?

Grabbit: At this rate it's going to take years to finish this room. Come here, I'll show you how to do it. **(He gets a fresh roll of paper and unrolls it on to the table.)** Now, hold on to the end of that paper and don't you dare let go of it. I don't want it rolling all over the place.

(Runn holds the end of it by kneeling at the end of the table and holding the paper down with his fingers. His face is almost level with the paper. Grabbit pastes the paper without looking at what he is doing and pastes Runn's face as well. When this is done, Grabbit holds the paper up as if to put it on the wall but Runn pulls Grabbit's shirt from his waistband and wipes his face on it.)

Runn: I've got paste in my eyes now.

Grabbit: Well don't wipe it all over my shirt. I've got it from a catalogue and I was going to send it back.

Runn: Never mind your rotten shirt, I've got blooming paste everywhere and it's all your fault.

Grabbit: My fault?

Runn: Ah! Glad you admit it.

Grabbit: Idiot, if you've got paste everywhere then a little more won't hurt you, will it?

(Grabbit goes to the paste bucket and gets his hands full of paste. He walks towards Runn with his hands out as if to slap them in Runn's face but he claps his hands together causing the paste to go all over him. Grabbit goes back to the bucket and gets another handful of paste and rubs it in Runn's face. Runn picks up a bucket of paste and pours it into Grabbit's trousers. Grabbit takes Runn's bowler hat and fills it with paste. There is a small hole in the top of the hat so as he forces the hat down on to Runn's head the paste squirts out of the top. Black-out.)

Icing the Cake Routine

This slosh routine was written by us for a theatre company who were performing a variety show. They wanted a good old fashioned pantomime slosh routine to put in their show. The beauty of this routine is that it is not as messy or expensive as the previous one.

(Granary enters Right, followed by Huntley and Palmer, they are arguing. Palmer is pushing a shopping trolley.)

Palmer: Yea but…

Huntley: No but…

Granary: Stop arguing you two. We'll soon be at the palace. I have a great plan to cheer up the King - he'll be happy as a Prince.

Huntley: How can you be so sure?

Granary: Well it so happens that I have a plan up my sleeve.

Huntley: } **(Together, looking up her sleeves.)**

Palmer: } What plan?

Granary: We are going to present him with a beautiful big birthday cake.

Huntley: Birthday cake?

Palmer:	Where are you going to get a birthday cake from?
Huntley:	It may have escaped your notice, but we're miles from anywhere.
Granary:	I made one last night – all we have to do is decorate it.
Huntley:	} **(Together.)**
Palmer:	} Decorate it - where?
Granary:	Here - right here.
Jenny:	But we're in the middle of the forest.
Granary:	Yes, but I'm clever I am. **(Gives a big false smile.)** I've bought all the stuff with me **(points to the shopping trolley)** right there.
Palmer:	You bought them? Huh! It was *me* pushing that trolley over hill, over dell, thorough bush, thorough brier…
Granary:	**(As though ad-libbing.)** Stick to Pantomime my boy, Shakespeare isn't for you.
Huntley:	**(Pointing to Palmer.)** Yes, he should be bard.
Granary:	Now let's see what we've got.

(Granary goes to the trolley and takes out a plastic table cloth and gives it to Huntley and Palmer who spread it on the ground, up stage Left. Granary then takes out the cake.)

Granary:	There you are, isn't it a beauty? Well, it will be when we've iced it.
Huntley:	Mmmm, it looks great.
Palmer:	Can we have a piece, please?
Granary:	No you can't it's for the King. **(She puts the cake on the cloth.)** Now get some plates out to put the icing on.

(Huntley gets the small pile of paper plates out and gives them to Palmer.)

Palmer:	Oh look, flying saucers. **(He spins about two or three plates out into the Audience like Frisbees.)**

(Huntley then takes out a tin of squirty cream and a cherry, and takes them over to the cloth and puts them down next to the cake.)

Granary: Stop that at once and bring them here. I need them to put the icing on them.

(Palmer gives the paper plates to Granary, who puts three of them out on the cloth.)

Granary: Huntley - bring me that bowl of icing.

Huntley: Yes Mumsy. **(He gets the bowl of foam mixture out of the trolley and takes it towards the Audience. He gives a little trip as though he is about to spill it onto the Audience.)** Whoops! **(He takes the bowl over to Granary who puts it down next to the cake.)**

Granary: And now put some of the icing on the plates.

(Huntley uses his hands and slops foam onto the three plates. When he has finished, he looks at his dirty messy hands, then looks up at Palmer.)

Huntley: Palmer can you come here a minute.

Palmer: **(He goes over to Huntley.)** Yes, what do you want?

Huntley: I want clean hands. **(He wipes his hands clean of Palmer's clothes.)**

Palmer: Oy, what did you do that for?

(Palmer gets a handful of foam and wipes it on Huntley.)

Palmer: Take that!

Huntley: Ugh – I'll get you for that.

Granary: Boys, boys. Will you stop that at once? The icing is supposed to go on the cake not each other. Now take a plate each and let's ice the cake.

(Granary, Huntley and Palmer each pick up a plate of foam. Granary sniffs her plate.)

Granary: Mmmm, this smells nice.

Palmer: **(Sniffs his plate.)** Mmmm.

(Granary knocks Palmer so his face goes into his plate of foam. Huntley starts laughing at Palmer.)

Huntley: **(Pointing at Palmer.)** Ha ha, look at you. You look like the icing on the cake.

(Palmer pushes Huntley's face into his plate of foam and laughs at him.)

Palmer: Now who's got an-ice face?

(Huntley and Palmer start a girly slappy-hand fight with ad-libbed dialogue such as "You horror" – "How dare you" etc.)

Granary: Now stop that at once. **(She points to the plates.)** Palmer - more icing please.

(Palmer uses his hands to top up the icing on the three plates. He then looks at his messy hands and wipes them on Huntley. Huntley and Palmer start their girly slappy-hand fight all over again. Granary pushes them apart, puts her hands into the foam then wipes them on Huntley and Palmer's faces.)

Granary: There - now get on with icing that cake or we'll be late getting to the palace.

(Huntley looks at Palmer; both give each other a little nod, pick up a plate of foam each and stand each side of Granary. They go to slap the plates of foam into Granary's face, but she steps back and they get each other's faces.)

Palmer: Ugh! That's not fair, you moved.

Granary: **(Laughs.)** That'll teach you. You'll never get one over on me.

(Huntley and Palmer wipe their hands and faces on each other's clothes.)

Granary: Right, the fun is over; now get on with icing the cake will you.

(Granary, Huntley and Palmer all cover the cake in foam. They all stand back and admire it.)

Granary: That looks wonderful. **(She turns round to Huntley and Palmer with her back to the cake.)** Look at the state of you two. The Palace moat is just over there, go and have a good wash and get cleaned up.

(Huntley and Palmer both look at each other, nod then give Granary a push. She falls backwards and sits down on top of the iced cake. Huntley picks up the squirty cream and squirts it all over Granary's head. Palmer picks up the cherry and puts it artistically on top of the cream. Huntley and Palmer then give each other a High five and quickly exit Left.)

Granary: (**Getting up.**) Why, you little… come back here. (**She runs off after them.**)

Fig 5 - *Helen Ford, Colin Pritchard, and Tom Hopgood with the Icing The Cake Routine.*

~~~~(**D**)~~~~

The Wages Routine

This is a great routine that can be used time and time again in different scripts, as long as it is written from a different angle each time. It can be used in Dick Whittington with Idle Jack and the Alderman, or it can be used in almost any pantomime using the Comedy Duo or the Comic Lead on the receiving end.

(**Jasper and Casper are on stage. There is a blackboard behind them. The Squire enters.**)

Jasper: (**Big he-man attitude.**) Hey Squire, we've been having a little discussion, and I have something to say to you.

Squire: Really, and what exactly would you like to say?

Jasper: (**Weakening under the Squire's gaze.**) Well, it's like this, I was thinking – no, *we* were thinking, er, I mean, (**points to Casper**) Casper was thinking... (**To Casper.**) You tell him what *you* were thinking.

Casper: Me?

Jasper: Yes, you.

Squire: Come along, speak up – I haven't got all day you know.

Jasper: Tell him, tell him, tell him.

Casper: No, no, no.

Jasper: Yes, yes, yes.

Casper: Well, er... It's... it's about time you paid us our wages.

Squire: (**Blustering.**) Do what?

Casper: We've worked for you for a whole year, so we deserve to get paid for it.

Squire: But you didn't *do* any work last year.

Casper: What do you mean; we didn't do any work last year?

Jasper: We worked our fingers to the bone for you.

Casper: And all we've got to show for it is bony fingers.

Squire: Huh! I'll show you. (**Takes a piece of chalk from his pocket.**) How many days in a year? (**He moves over to the blackboard.**)

Jasper: } (**Together.**)

Casper: } Three hundred and sixty-five

Squire: Assuming it's a leap year?

Jasper: (**Pleased with himself.**) Three hundred and sixty-six.

Squire: (**Writes 366 on the board.**) How many hours do you work each day?

Jasper: } (**Together, counting on their fingers.**)

Casper: } Eight hours.

Squire: There's twenty-four hours in a day but you only work eight, that's a third of the day - so that means you only work a third of the time. A third of three hundred and sixty-six, is one hundred and twenty-two. **(Crosses out the 366, and writes 122 on the board.)** Now, you don't work Sunday's do you?

Jasper: } **(Together, shaking their heads.)**

Casper: } No

Squire: There are fifty-two Sunday's in the year. Fifty-two from a hundred and twenty-two, let me think, that leaves seventy... **(Crosses out the 122, and writes 70 below it.)**

Jasper: Here, hang on a minute.

Casper: That's not fair.

Squire: ... And you don't work Saturday's either do you?

Jasper: } **(Together, in disbelief.)**

Casper: } No.

Squire: Fifty-two Saturdays - take that away, and that makes eighteen. **(He writes it down.)**

Jasper: Hey, steady on.

Squire: How many bank holidays do I let you have off each year?

Jasper: } **(Together.)**

Cassper: } Four days

Squire: Four from eighteen - that makes fourteen. **(He writes 14 on the board.)**

Jasper: **(A little angry.)** You rogue.

Squire: Tut, tut – temper, temper.

Casper: **(Shrugs shoulders.)** Well at least we will still get fourteen days' pay.

Squire: That's what you think. Did you have a holiday last year?

Jasper: Yes.

Casper: We went to Brighton for two weeks.

Squire: Two weeks?

Jasper: Two weeks.

Squire: That's fourteen days. Fourteen from fourteen is nought. **(He crosses out the 14, and writes a large 0.)** So you didn't do any work last year. No work, no pay.

~~~~(**D**)~~~~

Cuppa Tea Routine

Here is a nice little routine that we devised especially for our pantomime, *'Jack and Jill'*. We had Brown Owl and Akela, the Comic Duo, doing the routine. This piece can be adapted to suit almost any pantomime script.

(Brown Owl and Akela are at the palace and they are offered a cup of tea by the King, who has gone to fetch it.)

Akela: It's very posh here.

Brown Owl: Don't you go showing me up.

Akela: Me? It's more likely to be the other way round.

Brown Owl: How dare you.

Akela: What shall I do when I get my cuppa? I don't know how to drink tea like posh people.

Brown Owl: You're right, I've never known anyone slurp like you. **(Sudden thought.)** I've got an idea. When the King gets the tea, we'll do what he does.

Akela: You mean, copy him?

Brown Owl: We'll follow him exactly – whatever he does, we do then we can't go wrong.

Akela: That's not a bad idea.

(King returns with tea, so they mimic everything he does. First he blows in the cup, then leans back and lets out a sigh, they copy him. The King then pours some tea in his saucer; Brown Owl and Akela look at each other, shrug their shoulders and do the same. The King then dips his finger in the saucer of tea, winces and shakes his finger because the tea was hot, they both copy him. The King then blows on the tea in the saucer and they do the same. After that, the King takes

a small but noisy sip of tea from the saucer and rolls it round in his mouth as though checking it. They copy him)

King: Ahh. **(He licks his lips then puts his saucer on the floor.)**

Akela: Ahh.

Brown Owl: Bisto.

(Brown Owl and Akela lick their lips and put their saucers on the floor.)

King: **(Getting up and calling out)** Here kitty kitty, where are you. I've got a nice saucer of tea for you.

(Brown Owl and Akela look at each other aghast.)

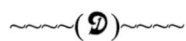

The Pendant Routine

This little corker, also known as the Dingle-Dangle routine, has been a great routine for many years, but hasn't shown up in many scripts recently. It can be used in the majority of pantomimes quite easily. When this routine was used in *'The Pied Piper'* by Bob Heather, it was changed to a five pound note which the Dame put in her cleavage for safety while the Comic Duo were trying to vie for her charms.

(Grabbit and Runn are on-stage. Sarah enters Right.)

Grabbit: Wow, look at her all dolled up to the nines, I wouldn't mind taking her to the dance.

Runn: I saw her first.

Grabbit: Didn't.

Runn: Did.

Grabbit: Huh, you stand no chance with her.

Runn: I've got a better chance than you.

(Grabbit and Run start slapping at each other.)

Sarah: **(To the Audience.)** Well, there seems to be some competition to take me out dancing.

(Sarah separates Grabbit and Runn with comic effect.)

Sarah: Boys, boys! I know what we'll do. We'll have a contest to woo me. The one who woos me the best can take me out tonight.

Grabbit: **(To the Audience.)** There's no competition. She's mine already.

Runn: You think a lot of yourself; it'll be me that takes her out tonight, not you.

Sarah: **(She starts twirling and playing with her pendant.)** What do you think of my sparkley?

Grabbit: } **(Together.)**

Runn: } Your what?

Sarah: My sparkley – my pendulous. The one that wins, not only gets to take me out, but gets my sparkley as well.

Grabbit: This should be a walkover.

Sarah: **(She pops the pendant back into her cleavage, then to Grabbit.)** Right young man, you can go first.

Grabbit: **(To Runn, pushing him out of the way.)** I'll show you who's best. **(To Sarah.)** Well, as I am a debonair sort of chap. I would take your hand like this **(he does so)** and I would say**, (in a mock French accent)** "My 'ow wonderful you look today, may I kees your 'and?" **(He kisses her hand.)**

Sarah: Oh wonderful.

Grabbit: **(He then smells the air round her.)** Mmm! 'Ow nice you smell.

Sarah: Yes, it's Cillit Bang.

Grabbit: May I kiss you on zee cheek?

Sarah: If you must. **(She starts to turn and bend.)**

Grabbit: **(He taps his own cheek.)** No! - Your cheek.

Sarah: Oh silly me.

(Grabbit kisses Sarah on the cheek.)

Grabbit: Then I would say "Madamselle, would you do me the honour of letting me escort you to the discotheque tonight?

Sarah: **(With a sensual shudder.)** Woooo, that's wonderful. Oh I say you really know how to woo a girl.

(Sarah turns to Runn and runs her finger up his arm.)

Sarah: Now it's your turn, sunshine.

Grabbit: (**Cockily, dropping the French accent.**) Let's see you beat that.

Runn: Right. Here goes. - Hiya sexy. Do you fancy going to the disco with me?

(Runn pounces on Sarah and grabs her roughly in a comical, clumsy embrace trying to kiss her. While they are locked together, Runn takes the pendant from Sarah, without the Audience seeing.)

Sarah: Help!! Unhand me.

(Sarah finally manages to pull away from Runn. She is looking somewhat dishevelled, and is gasping for air.)

Sarah: What are you trying to do? – Smother me?

(Sarah pushes Runn away from her and regains her posture.)

Sarah: Well obviously the one who wins me is the one with style and class. **(She turns to Grabbit.)** You are the one with all the charm. You win. **(Turning to Runn.)** I'm very sorry dear, but he's the one that gets me.

Grabbit: I got the girl, I got the girl.

Runn: Maybe, **(holding the pendant above his head)** but I got the pendant.

Sarah: Hey, give me back my sparkley.

Grabbit: Why, you little... Come back here.

~~~~($\mathcal{D}$)~~~~

The Drill Routine

This is a routine that has been in more pantomimes that anyone cares to remember, but if it is done right, it can still bring the house down in fits of uncontrollable laughter. This routine doesn't have to be set on deck of a ship, it could be used in the King's army. In our version of *'Old King Cole'*, it was set in the sweet shop belonging to Candy Floss, the Dame, using large candy canes instead of mops when she tried to train Old King Cole's Fiddlers-Three to become soldiers.

(Enter Bosun, Mate, Dame, and Billy. They are all carrying mops. They start mopping the decks. The Captain enters.)

Captain: Now then you lot. I think we ought to have some drill. We'll use those mops instead of weapons until you know what you're doing.

(Bosun, Mate, Dame, and Billy all groan.)

Captain: Right, you lot, fall in.

(Bosun, Mate, Dame, and Billy all rush to the side of the ship as if to jump overboard.)

Captain: What do you think you're doing?

Billy: You said fall in.

Captain: I didn't mean fall in over the side. I meant fall in over here, blockheads.

Bosun: Fall in here.

Mate: Fall in there.

Billy: I wish he'd make up his mind.

(They all mutter.)

Captain: Shut up. Now then, attenshun, at ease, shun ease, shun ease, shun ease.

Dame: **(Throwing down her mop.)** Steady on - I'm not an athlete you know.

Mate: I can see that.

Dame: Here, watch it mate.

Captain: **(Indicating her mop.)** Pick that up.

Dame: No.

Captain: Pick it up.

Dame: I said no.

Captain: Will you pick that up?

Dame: No I will not.

Captain: Please pick it up. Just for me.

Dame: **(Sweet smile.)** No.

Captain: Oh very well then, don't. **(He walks away, then suddenly turns and shouts.)** Pick it up.

(**The Mate jumps into the Bosun's arms. Billy picks up the mop and hands it to Dame who is now hiding behind the Bosun.**)

Captain: Get back in line. Now, stand at ease. Stand easy.

(**Billy leans on his mop with his legs apart. The Dame kicks the mop through his legs causing him to fall over.**)

Captain: What are you doing down there?

Billy: Getting up.

Captain: Get up and get in line. Now, from the right, number!

(**They all start dancing.**)

Captain: What do you think you're doing? I said number.

Bosun: Oh. We thought you said rumba.

Captain: Pay attention. From the right, number.

Billy: Two.

Dame: Two.

Bosun: Three.

Captain: That doesn't sound right – do it again?

Billy: Two.

Dame: Two

Bosun: Three.

Captain: (**To Billy.**) Aren't you one?

Billy: No, but I'm a bit worried about him. (**Points to Bosun.**)

Captain: Bah. Come along now. Squad - Close up.

(**Dame lifts up the front of her frock.**)

Captain: Not that way.

Dame: Oh, you mean this way. (**She turns round and lifts the back of her frock to reveal an 'L' plate sewn on the back of her bloomers.**)

Captain: Stand up woman. What do you think you are doing.

Dame: I was only doing what you said.

Captain: (**Holding his head.**) Twenty years at sea and I have never felt that sick before. Now, who knows anything about navigation?

Billy:	I do. My father was a navvy.
Captain:	Idiot boy. **(Short and sharp.)** Squad.
All:	**(Short and sharp.)** Yes.
Captain:	Squaaaaaaaaaaaaaaad!
All:	Yeeeeeeeeeeeeeeeees!
Captain:	Present arms!

(Dame, Mate, Bosun and Billy run over to the Captain and offer him the mops.)

Captain:	That's not how you present arms. I'll show you. **(He takes a mop from the Bosun.)** It's like this. **(He presents arms properly.)** One and two and three and four. **(He throws the mop on the floor.)** That's the way to do it. Now. Squad. Present arms!
All:	**(Together.)** One and two and three and four. **(They all throw their mops on the floor.)** That's the way to do it.
Captain:	Pick them up. Now then squad, shoulder arms.

(They shoulder arms but Dame puts her mop on the wrong shoulder to everyone else.)

| Captain: | No not on that shoulder, put it on this one. **(Pats his own left shoulder.)** |

(Dame puts her mop on the Captain's shoulder.)

| Captain: | Not there. Put it where he's got his. **(He points to the Bosun's shoulder.)** |

(The Dame now puts her mop on the Bosun's shoulder. The Captain grabs her mop from the Bosun's shoulder and puts it in position on her left shoulder. He is by now beside himself with rage and shouts at her.)

Bosun:	Put it there. Put it there.
Dame:	Well why didn't you say?
Captain:	**(To Bosun.)** If we were attacked at sea, what steps would you take?
Bosun:	Bloomin' great big ones.
Billy:	Wouldn't you get wet?
Bosun:	Not as wet as you, you big drip.
Billy:	Don't call me a drip.

Captain: None of you look as if you are fit enough to defend anyone. We'll do some exercises. Follow me. **(He runs on the spot.)** One two, one two, as if you were riding a bicycle. One two, one two, as if you were riding a bicycle.

All: **(Joining in running on the spot.)** One two, one two, as if you were riding a bicycle. One two, one two, as if you were riding a bicycle.

(The Dame stops and leans on her mop. The others carry on.)

Captain: What do you think you're doing?

Dame: I'm free-wheeling.

Captain: I knew it was bad luck to have a woman aboard. Squad attention.

(Everyone stands to attention.)

Captain: Left turn.

(Everyone turns left except for the Bosun who turns right and faces the Dame. She grabs her chance and gives him a quick kiss.)

Bosun: **(Turning the right way.)** Yuk and double yuk.

Captain Quiiiiiiiiiiiick ...

(Everyone anticipates his command and lift their legs ready to march.)

Captain: Wait for it. Wait for it. Quick march.

(Music plays. Everyone marches around the stage and salute the Audience as they exit. Billy doesn't see the others turn, and he walks into the pros arch on one side of the stage.)

The Echo Routine

This routine is an old favourite that can be used in almost any pantomime script and in any scene. It is another one of the gambling routines that always seem to work so well in vaudeville, variety shows, and pantomimes. This is ideal as a front-of-cloth filler while the set is being changed behind the curtain.

(Billy and Simon enter.)

Billy: Do you know I'm so broke that if ten pound notes were on sale at the Pound Shop for fifty pence each, I wouldn't be able to afford to buy any.

Simon: Well in that case you might be interested in my new idea for making money.

Billy: You've got an idea for making money? I'm all ears.

Simon: I know, but we can't all be perfect.

Billy: Never mind the cheek, what about this money?

Simon: Let me explain. First of all did you know there is an echo here?

Billy: Do what?

Simon: Did you know there's an echo here?

Billy: **(Looks around.)** I say, there's an echo here.

Simon: That's me.

Billy: Do what?

Simon: That's me.

Billy: There it is again.

Simon: Listen - there is *no* echo here.

Billy: But you just said there was.

Simon: I know I said there was but there isn't.

Billy: There isn't?

Simon: There isn't.

Billy: There it is again.

Simon: There's not an echo here really, but we tell people there is.

Billy: That's stupid

Simon: If we pretend there's an echo, we can make money out of people. It's simple.

Billy: I think you're the one that's simple. How can we make money by pretending there's an echo here?

Simon: I'll show you. Just stand over there, out of sight and repeat everything I say.

Billy: Just stand over there out of sight and repeat everything I say?

Simon: Not now you idiot, when I tell you. Now get over there.

(Billy goes off stage.)

Simon: Can you hear me?

Billy: **(Popping his head round the side.)** Yes, of course 1 can. I'm only over here.

Simon: Just keep out of sight and repeat everything I say.

Billy: I'm sorry. I didn't realize. **(He exits.)**

Simon: Can you hear me?

Billy: Can you hear me?

Simon: How are you?

Billy: **(Entering with a hobble.)** I've got this ingrowing toenail.

Simon: No, no, no. You stay out of sight and repeat everything I say.

Billy: Everything?

Simon: Everything.

Billy: There it is again.

Simon: No it's not, just do as I say.

Billy: I'm sorry. I think I've got it now. **(He exits.)**

Simon: Hello.

Billy: Hello.

Simon: How are you?

Billy: How are you?

Simon: My Uncle Fred has got a bad back.

Billy: **(Entering.)** You want to rub some deep heat on it, that'll get rid of it.

Simon: No, no, no. Will you just do as I say? **(He looks off.)** Quick, there's somebody coming - get out of sight and remember what I said.

Billy: All right, all right, I'm going.

(Billy exits. Dame enters from opposite side.)

Dame: Oh look, it's Simple Simon. How are you?

Simon: I'm very well but I'm a bit worried about this echo here.

Dame: What echo where?

Simon:	This echo here.
Dame:	What are you talking about, there's no echo here.
Simon:	Oh, but there is.
Dame:	Don't be silly, I know this place well. I used to do my courting here, if there was an echo I'd have had twice as much fun.
Simon:	Well I'll bet you ten pounds there is an echo here.
Dame:	Ten pounds - ok, prove it.
Simon:	Right. Listen to this. Hello.
Billy:	Hello.
Simon:	How are you?
Billy:	How are you?
Simon:	Oompa, oompa.
Billy:	Stick it up your jumper.
Dame:	That's very good but can I try it out?
Simon:	Yes of course you can.
Dame:	Hello.
Billy:	Hello.
Dame:	I am waiting for you.
Billy:	I am waiting for you.
Dame:	To come and get me.
Billy:	You must be joking.
Dame:	I know where...
Billy:	I know where…
Dame:	You can get…
Billy:	You can get…
Dame:	A big tub of chocolate ice cream….
Billy:	A big tub of chocolate ice cream…
Dame:	For nothing.
Billy:	**(Running on stage.)** Where? I love chocolate ice cream.

(Simon yells at Billy and chases off. Dame picks up the money, holds it up for Audience to see, then exits.)

The Kiss

This is a lovely short routine that can be used in almost any script between Principal Boy and Principal Girl. It also works well as piece for Buttons and Cinders in Cinderella.

(Buttons looks into Cinders eyes.)

Buttons: Oh Cinders, would you like a little bet with me?

Cinders: A bet? What sort of a bet, Buttons?

Buttons: Well, this may sound silly, but I bet you a pound that I can kiss you on the lips without touching you.

Cinders: Oh Buttons, that's silly, it's impossible to kiss without touching.

Buttons: If you bet me a pound, I'll show you how it's done.

Cinders: But you *can't* kiss me without touching me?

Buttons: I bet I can. Close your eyes.

(Cinders closes her eyes and Buttons kisses her full on the lips, then falls flat on his back in ecstasy. Cinders reacts.)

Cinders: But you *did* touch me, Buttons.

Buttons: **(Getting up.)** Did I?

Cinders: Yes, you owe me a pound.

Buttons: Here's your pound **(big grin)** but boy, was it worth it!

Cinders: Oh Buttons.

(Cinders and Buttons exit laughing.)

The Lollipop Routine

Although this routine is short and sweet, it is a great little routine and can be used anywhere - although it often crops up in the schoolroom scene. It doesn't have to be a lollipop that is used - it can be a pound coin, penny, chocolate, or sweets.

(Sarah the dame and Billy are on stage together. Sarah has two lollipops in her hand.)

Sarah: Are you any good at sums?

Billy: Well – some sums seem easy and some sums seem hard.

Sarah: That's easy for you to say - I'd better test you.

Billy: Oh must you?

Sarah: If you've got one lollipop in this pocket... **(she puts a lollipop in Billy's jacket pocket)** and one in this pocket... **(she puts second lollipop in his other pocket)** then I take one away... **(she takes lollipop back out of one pocket)** how many lollipops have you got?

Billy: Two.

Sarah: No, no, no. You're not listening. I'll say it again. Give me back the lollipop.

Billy: I knew there'd be a catch. **(He gives her back the lollipop.)**

Sarah: If you've got one lollipop in this pocket... **(puts it in)** and one in this pocket... **(puts it in)** then I take one away... **(takes one out of pocket)** how many lollipops will you have?

Billy: Two.

Sarah: **(She stamps her foot.)** No, no, no. How can you have two if I've just taken one away?

Billy: Because I've already got a lollipop in this pocket.

(Billy pulls a lollipop out of his trouser pocket.)

~~~(𝒟)~~~

The Mirror Routine

This routine is a wonderful addition to any pantomime, but it does need a lot of rehearsing as the details need to be spot-on at all times. There is a large opening at the rear of the stage to represent the mirror frame. This should either be parallel to the stage or set at a very slight angle to it. There should be nothing behind the frame with the exception of a black or silver curtain.

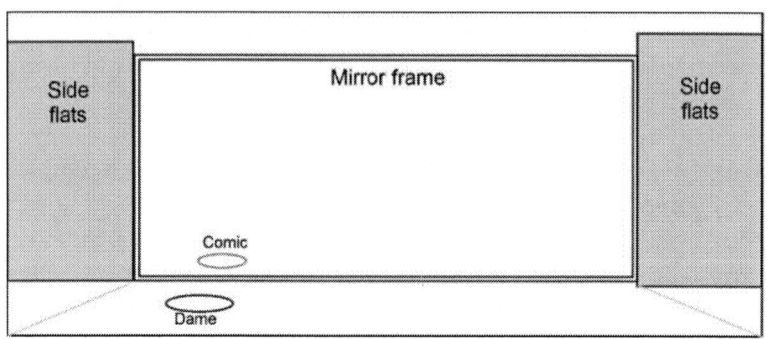

Fig 6 - *The stage set for the Mirror routine. View from the front.*

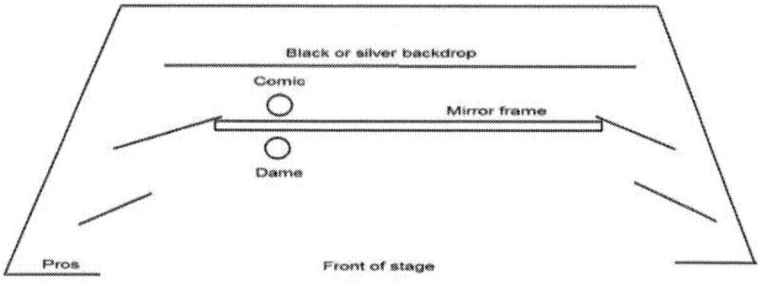

Fig 7 - *The stage set for the Mirror routine. View from above.*

The routine starts with the Dame coming on stage and says a few words to the Audience about looking her best. She then moves back to the side of the stage again and turns to look in the mirror. As she turns, the Comic appears behind the mirror frame dressed exactly the same as the Dame. The Comic mirrors everything the Dame does. It must be remembered that when the Dame moves her left arm, leg, or whatever, the Comic should move his right to give the correct visual impact.

The whole routine starts with nice simple moves like tidying her hair, brushing her cheek etc. with the Comic mimicking her every move until there is a point where the Dame notices a mark on the mirror, so she puts her hand out to the invisible mark and the Comic does the same so their hands are touching, they then proceed to polish together, even to the point where they both 'huff' onto the mirror and polish it together.

You can add many ideas to this and it is always guaranteed to raise a laugh. The routine can end in several ways such as the Dame finally brushing herself down and making her exit, mirrored by the Comic. Or you can perform it with a catch-out finish. This is achieved by the Comic being caught out by the Dame by doing something different.

There is an old film clip with Harpo Marks and Lucille Ball doing this routine and it finishes with Harpo taking off his hat, mirrored by Miss Ball, he then drops it. The only difference is that Harpo has a piece of elastic on his hat and therefore it springs back up for him to catch. It is always worth checking this out on YouTube, along with other versions of the routine.

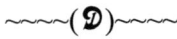

The Pheasant Routine

This has always been an old favourite with amateur and professional pantomime writers everywhere. When we used this routine in our version of *'Treasure Island'*, we changed it from a pheasant to a lobster, to fit in with the nautical flavour of the show.

(Tom enters Right carrying a bag with the tail feathers of a pheasant sticking out. There is also a letter in the bag.)

Tom: (**To Audience.**) I've just received a present from my granny. (**Tom looks in the bag then looks up again with a big grin on his face.**) Wow! It's a pheasant. (**He looks in the bag again and takes out a letter.**) Oh, she's put a letter in there as well. (**Reads.**) It says I hope you enjoy this gift of a nice pheasant. (**Looks in the bag again and takes a huge sniff.**) Phew, it stinks, (**grimaces at the smell.**) it must have gone off in the post. I'll have to get rid of this as soon as I can. I wonder who I can give it to.

(**Jerry enters Left. Tom puts the letter in his pocket.**)

Tom: Well, well, well, the very person.

Jerry: Hello. What have you got there?

Tom: Oh I'd like to give you a pheasant as a pleasant present.

Jerry: That's easy for you to say.

(**Tom hands the bag to Jerry.**)

Jerry: Why, thank you very much, that's very kind of you.

(**Tom exits Right laughing.**)

Jerry: I love pheasant. (**Looks in the bag. Immediately the smell hits him.**) Cor, what a rotten stink, it's gone orf. I must get rid of this – and the sooner the better.

(**Rosie enters Right.**)

Rosie: Oh how exciting, first thing tomorrow we're off on an adventure. Just what the doctor ordered – a lov-erly trip in the sunshine with the Captain. (**Spots Jerry.**) Hello, I didn't see you there - have you been shopping?

Jerry: No - er, yes. Actually I brought this for you. It's a present.

Rosie: A present - for little old me?

Jerry: Yes it's a pheasant; I thought you might like it for your supper. (**Hands it over then quickly exits Left.**)

Rosie: A present of a pheasant, how very kind. I'll make a nice pheasant casserole with it for the Squire and me. (**Opens the bag and sticks her nose in.**) Lummy, what a pong – it's off. I must get rid of this as quickly as I can.

(Billy enters Left.)

Billy: (Gives Rosie a little sniff.) Hello, have you been to the *[local]* tip?

Rosie: No I haven't. I've been to the market to buy you a little gift.

Billy: What is it?

Rosie: It's a pheasant, (hands it over to him) and I hope you'll both be very happy together. (Exits Right.)

Billy: A pheasant. I've never eaten pheasant before. (Scratches his head.) I wonder how you cook it - I think I'll have it with chips. (Opens the bag and gets a whiff.) Bloomin' heck, this one's already had its chips - it smells as if it hasn't changed its socks for a year. I'd better get rid of it somewhere.

(Billy exits Left, as Tom enters Right.)

Tom: (To Audience holding up the letter.) I've just been reading this letter from my granny. She says she's put a five pound note under the pheasant. I must try to get it back.

(Jerry enters Left.)

Tom: Have you got that pheasant I gave you?

Jerry: No, it was rotten, I gave it away.

Tom: Well my granny said she had put a fiver under it. I need to get it back.

Jerry: I gave it to Rosie.

(Rosie enters Right.)

Jerry: Ah, here she is now. Have you got that pheasant I gave you?

Rosie: No I haven't. It smelt 'orrible. Why do you ask?

Jerry: It's got a fiver under it. We must try to get it back.

Rosie: Oh heck, I gave it to Billy.

(Billy enters Left holding the bag with pheasant in it.)

Rosie: Thank goodness, here he is. (Snatches the bag from Billy.) I've got the pheasant.

Jerry: (Snatches the bag from Rosie.) I've got the pheasant.

Tom: (Snatches the bag from Jerry.) I've got the pheasant.

Billy: (Holding up a five pound note.) Yes, but I've got the fiver.

(Billy runs round the stage to the tune of Yakety-Sax with Rosie, Tom, and Jerry all chasing him. They all exit Left.)

The Pound Routine

The pound routine is ideal as a filler in a front-of-cloth scene. Whatever happens, the singer should carry on regardless with his song, not flinching and dead-pan the whole way through the song. He should take no notice of the duo and never look at them during their escapade. This started life many years ago as the shilling routine, but due to inflation the routine has gone up in price.

(The Squire enters.)

Squire: Ladies and gentlemen. I have had a request from many of you to sing a lovely old song entitled *[title]*.

(Own choice of music-hall song. The Squire starts to sing the song and throughout the song and everything that follows, he must keep a deadpan expression on his face and ignore completely everything that goes on around him. On no account must he stop singing. Freddy and Teddy enter.)

Freddy: Well what have you brought me here for?

Teddy: I've lost a pound coin and I'm sure this is where I lost it. Could you to help me find it?

Freddy: (Searching around the stage.) Well I can't see anything here.

Teddy: (Indicating where the Squire is.) I wonder if he's got it.

Freddy: He might - perhaps we ought to search him.

Teddy: A good idea. Let's have a look.

(Teddy and Freddy start searching the Squire who carries on singing and totally ignores them. They take off his hat and look under it. Then remove his jacket and search that. They lift his arms to look underneath and search his trouser pockets etc. They can even look in his mouth if he happens to be singing a long note.)

Freddy: Well he hasn't got it, has he?

Teddy: I've just had a thought; I wonder if I dropped it in the orchestra pit. Let's have a look.

Freddy: If you did, they have probably spent it in the bar by now. You know what musicians are like?

(Teddy and Freddy go into the orchestra pit to search it. They go around the musicians pulling out all manner of strange objects. A flask, a pair of false teeth (as though from taken from a musician's mouth), an old bra, a half-eaten doughnut - anything that will bring a laugh.)

Freddy: It's not here is it? Are you sure this is where you dropped it?

Teddy: (Points to auditorium.) I suppose I could have dropped it out there. Let's go and have a look.

(The house lights come on as Freddy and Teddy go amongst the Audience causing as much mayhem as possible. They can make a row of the Audience stand up whilst they search. They look under seats, in people's hats and kiddie's sweet packets etc. They do anything to cause total chaos.)

Freddy: Well it's not here anywhere. Perhaps we'd better look in the bar.

Teddy: Ok, let's go and see if we can find it there.

(Freddy and Teddy exit through the auditorium. The song comes to an end. The Squire bows to the Audience, then moves his foot to reveal the pound coin. He bends down and picks it up, kisses it, winks at the Audience, puts the coin in his pocket, and exits.)

The Parcel Routine

For a really funny routine, this is must be one of the tops. It can be used to its best effect as a front-of-cloth scene in order to give the stage crew time to change the scenery. Always guaranteed a laugh.

(The Duchess enters Right she is carrying a parcel. The parcel should contain several pieces of broken crockery, or something that rattles a lot, and should be packed in a good strong box.)

Duchess: Oh hello. I've just got to take this parcel down to the post office. I think it's just outside the palace gates.

(Butler enters Left.)

Butler: Hello, where are you heading for?

Duchess: I'm just going to the post office; I've got to catch the post.

Butler: What is it?

Duchess: It's a twenty-eight piece dinner service.

Butler: A twenty-eight piece dinner service? I wouldn't send that by post if I were you.

Duchess: Why not?

Butler: I'll show you what happens. The postman takes the parcel from you and throws it in his sack. **(He takes parcel from the Duchess and drops it on the floor.)** Then he throws the sack over his shoulder **(he picks up the parcel and throws it over his shoulder)** just like this. Then when it gets to the sorting office, they stamp it like this.

(The Butler picks up the parcel from the floor and bashes it with the side of his fist.)

Butler: Then they throw it in another sack to deliver it. **(Throws parcel over his shoulder.)** I wouldn't send it by post if I was you - after all you wouldn't want to get it damaged at all, would you? **(He exits Right.)**

Duchess: Oh dear. No, I wouldn't want it damaged.

(As she picks up the parcel, the Chancellor enters Left.)

Chancellor: What have you got there?

Duchess: It's a… **(she shakes the parcel)** … fifty-eight piece dinner service. I was going to post it, but then something made me decide to send it by airmail.

Chancellor: Oh, I wouldn't send it by airmail.

Duchess: Why ever not - what's wrong with airmail?

Chancellor: I'll show you. **(He takes the Duchess's parcel.)** When a parcel goes by airmail, the man on the ground throws it into the plane. **(He throws parcel across the stage.)** Then the airplane hits some turbulence and the parcels get shaken about. **(He picks up the parcel and runs around making a noise like an aeroplane. He then shakes the parcel vigorously.)** That doesn't sound to good does it? Then when the plane gets to the end of the flight, the man in the plane throws it to the man on the ground. **(He throws the parcel to the floor.)** So I wouldn't send it by airmail. After all, you wouldn't want to crack a saucer would you? **(He exits.)**

Duchess: No, I wouldn't want to get any of them cracked.

(The Duchess picks up the parcel. The King enters Left.)

King: Hello Duchess. What's that you've got there?

Duchess: It's a… **(she gives it another shake)** …ninety-six piece dinner service. It's a present for someone so I've decided to send it by boat.

King: Oh dear. You can't send a fragile parcel like that by boat.

Duchess: I don't know why I shouldn't, but I have a feeling that you're going to show me.

King: Well if you want me to. **(He takes the parcel from her.)** When a parcel goes by boat, the man on the shore throws it to the man on the boat.

Duchess: I somehow thought he might.

King: But the boat is rocking badly and the man misses it just like this.

(The King throws the parcel at Duchess, but misses her.)

Duchess: Careful your highness, you nearly hit me with it and that would never do.

King: Then the man on the boat picks it up to take it to the hold, but on his way, he trips over the anchor chain and drops it. **(He picks the parcel up, trips across the stage and drops the parcel again.)** Then when he gets to the hold, he drops it in. **(He drops the parcel from above head height.)** But it lands on the foot of the man down the hold and he isn't very happy.

Duchess: I didn't think he would be. So what happens next?

King: The man in the hold kicks it, **(he kicks the parcel, then hobbles around holding his foot)** then when the boat gets to the other end, the man in the hold throws it up to the man on the deck. **(He picks up parcel and throws it again.)** The man on the deck throws it to the man on the dock. **(He throws the parcel up into the air and lets it land on the stage.)** And the man on the dock throws it into the van so it can be delivered. **(Throws the parcel again.)** So I wouldn't send it by boat if I were you. You wouldn't want to get it chipped would you?

Duchess: Oh no that would never do. **(She picks up the parcel.)**

King: What did you say it was in the parcel?

Duchess: It's a **(shakes parcel)** five hundred piece dinner service.

King: Well if it's a fragile thing like that you ought to be careful with it.

Duchess: But I have been really careful with it.

King: Are you sure?

Duchess: Very sure.

King: I've got an idea. Why don't you deliver it personally?

Duchess: What a good idea. I think I will.

King: Who is it for anyway?

Duchess: It is a rather expensive wedding present that I bought especially for you.

(The Duchess hands the parcel to the King and exits Left.)

King: Oh dear, oh dear, oh dear. I'm going to have to go into the village now and buy a tube of glue. **(He exits Right with the parcel.)**

Fig 8 - *Colin Russell as King Cuthbert and Heather Whitham as the Duchess of Hydrangea from 'The King's New Clothes' by Peter Bond and Bob Heather.*

Who's The Bosun?

This little gem started life as an Abbot and Costello routine about baseball, "Who's on first base." We have now re-written the routine for pantomime use, it can be changed quite easily for different pantomimes. We have set this version at sea.

(Captain Cod and Mullet are on stage.)
Mullet: Glad we managed to get a new crew, Captain.
Cod: Ah yes, they be a wonderful bunch.

Mullet:	I don't suppose you know their names?
Cod:	Yes - Hoo is the Bosun, Watt is the cabin boy, and Ida No, the cook.
Mullet:	I thought you said you knew the crew's names.
Cod:	I'm telling you, Hoo is the Bosun, Watt is the cabin boy and Ida No the cook.
Mullet:	You're supposed to be in charge of this ship aren't you - yet you can't remember the crew's names.
Cod:	Of course I can, I've been friends with them all for more years than I care to remember.
Mullet:	**(Anger setting in.)** Then tell me their names.
Cod:	I told you, Hoo is the Bosun and Watt is the cabin boy.
Mullet:	**(Getting angrier.)** Look, let's make this easier – who is the Bosun?
Cod:	That's right.
Mullet:	I want to know his name.
Cod:	Hoo.
Mullet:	The Bosun.
Cod:	Hoo is the Bosun.
Mullet:	What are you asking me for?
Cod:	No, that's it. Hoo is the Bosun?
Mullet:	**(Getting angrier.)** I don't know.
Cod:	Ida No is the cook. Hoo is the Bosun.
Mullet:	Don't keep asking me – they're your friends. All I want to do is find out their names. Just tell me what is the name of the Bosun?
Cod:	No Watt's the name of the cabin boy
Mullet:	I'm not asking you who's the cabin boy?
Cod:	No, Hoo's the Bosun
Mullet:	That's what I keep asking you.
Cod:	And I keep telling you – Hoo's the Bosun.
Mullet:	You're a mighty fine captain if you don't know who's the Bosun.
Cod:	I know who's the Bosun.
Mullet:	Then what's his name?

Cod:	No, Watt is the cabin boy. Hoo is the Bosun
Mullet:	I don't know.
Cod:	Ida No is the cook.
Mullet:	Why are we talking about the cook?
Cod:	Because you mentioned her name.
Mullet:	I didn't mention anybody's name.
Cod:	Yes you did.
Mullet:	No I didn't.
Cod:	Yes you did.
Mullet:	No I didn't – just tell me what is the name of the Bosun?
Cod:	No, Watt is the name of the cabin boy?
Mullet:	**(Really frustrated by now.)** Don't keep asking me all these questions.

(Hoo enters.)

Mullet:	Who's this?
Cod:	That's right - he's the Bosun.
Mullet:	Who's the Bosun?
Cod:	He is.

(Watt enters.)

Mullet:	**(Points to Watt.)** And what is his name?
Cod:	That's right.
Mullet:	What's right?
Watt:	Yes, I'm always right.
Mullet:	Who's asking you?
Hoo:	No I wasn't – you were.
Mullet:	I'm getting so confuddled here.
Cod:	Let me explain one more time. **(Points to Bosun.)** He is the Bosun and his name is Hoo. **(Points to Watt.)** And he is the cabin boy and his name is Watt.
Mullet:	Ah, I'm beginning to see the light. He's the Bosun and his name is Hoo. He is the cabin boy and his name is Watt.
Cod:	By jove he's got it.

~~~~(*D*)~~~~

The Drink Of Truth

This little routine can be used almost anywhere in the script, and by almost any pair of characters, whether it is the comic duo or the leading comic and dame. It is also one of those rare routines that can even be played by two Chorus members.

Billy: I have here in this bottle a very special drink.

Joe: You don't mean a strawberry milk shake, do you?

Billy: No. This is even more special than a strawberry milk shake. It's called the drink of truth.

Joe: The drink of truth?

Billy: Yup – the drink of truth. One swig from this bottle and you can't help but tell the truth.

Joe: Has James Bond heard about this?

Billy: It was him who gave it to me.

Joe: Does it work?

Billy: One gulp and you're gullible.

Joe: I must have a go. **(He takes the bottle, drinks, and immediately spits it out.)**

Joe: That's vinegar.

Billy: I said you'd tell the truth.

(Billy is chased off by Joe.)

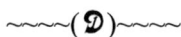

The Drinky Tree

We always tend to fall about with laughter at a person on stage, television, or film, who slips on a banana skin, gets covered in flour, receives a custard pie in the face, or gets squirted with water. It seems that we like to get our laughs from other people's misfortunes. The Drinky Tree routine is no exception as it relies on gullible characters getting a little bit damp for the Audience to enjoy.

Billy: Slow down Squire, we've been walking for ages now, I'm tired and thirsty - I could drink a lake.

Squire: That's handy because we're right next to the Drinky Tree?

Billy: The what-ey tree?

Squire: The Drinky Tree. It's magic - if ever you are thirsty just ask the tree and it'll give you a drink.

Billy: I don't believe you.

Squire: Why don't you try it? All you have to do is stand by the tree and say, "Drinky Tree, Drinky Tree, have you a nice little drink for me?" And you'll get it.

Billy: I'll get it?

Simon: You'll get it.

Billy: That sounds good, I'll try it. Now what do I say?

Squire: Drinky Tree, Drinky Tree, have you a nice little drink for me?

Billy: Oh yes, that's right. **(He goes up to tree.)** Drinky Tree, Drinky Tree, have you a nice little drink for me?

(Water squirts out from the tree all over Billy. The Squire exits laughing.)

Billy: Ahh, I'm all wet through now.

(Simon enters.)

Simon: Hello. What's the matter with you?

Billy: Oh nothing. It's just rather hot and I've started to sweat.

Simon: You're right, it is very hot today, and I'm so thirsty.

Billy: I can help you out there. This tree is a magic tree and if you ask it nicely it'll give you a drink.

Simon: Will it really? Where's the slot for the money?

Billy: No it's not a drinks machine – it's a magic tree.

Simon: What do I have to do?

Billy: Just stand here and say, "Drinky Tree, Drinky Tree, have you a nice little drink for me?" And you'll get it.

Simon: I'll get it will I?

Billy: Oh, you'll get it all right.

Simon: That's great. I'll have a go at that. Drinky Tree, Drinky Tree, have you a nice little drink for me?

(Water squirts over Simon. Billy exits laughing.)

Simon: That wasn't very nice. I'm going to get my own back on someone.

(Nursie enters.)

Nursie: At last. I thought I'd never get here. I wish I'd packed a bottle of beer.

Simon: If it's a drink you're after I think I can help you there.

Nursie: Have you got a bottle hidden about your person?

Simon: No, but I've got a magic tree.

Nursie: A magic tree. Where have you hidden that? **(She looks in Simon's pocket.)**

Simon: I haven't hidden it anywhere - it's there. **(Points to tree.)** If you stand next to it and say "Drinky Tree, Drinky Tree, have you a nice little drink for me?" you'll get it.

Nursie: If I say it twice will I get a double?

Simon: Oh don't worry. You'll get plenty.

Nursie: I'll have a try. Drinky Tree, Drinky Tree, have you a nice little drink for me?

(Nursie gets the water squirted all over her. Simon exits.)

Nursie: What a mess – I feel as though I've just had a bed-bath. Wait till I get my hands on that scoundrel.

(Squire enters.)

Squire: What's happened to you?

Nursie: Nothing's happened to me.

Squire: But you're all wet – have you been swimming? **(Idea.)** Hey, that's a good idea; I think I'll go for a swim in the river myself. **(He goes to exit.)**

Nursie: Before you go, would you like a drink with me?

Squire: No thanks, I'm not thirsty.

Nursie: Oh but you must be – it's very hot today. Come along, have a little drinky-winky with little ol' me.

Squire: **(He winks at the Audience.)** All right then.

Nursie: Good. All you have to do is stand next to this magic tree and say, "Drinky Tree, Drinky Tree, have you a nice little drink for me?" And you'll get it.

Squire: I'll get it, will I?

Nursie: Oh yes, you'll get it all right. Now come along, let's hear it.

Squire: Dinky Dee, Dinky Dee **(he steps forward)** have you a nice little drink for me?

(Nothing happens.)

Nursie: No, no, no. You got it wrong – it's Drinky Tree, not Dinky Dee.

Squire: Oh sorry, I'll try again. **(He stands next to the tree.)** Stinky Tree. Stinky Tree, have you a nice little drink for me?

(Still nothing. Nursie is getting angry now.)

Nursie: No, no, no - not Stinky Tree – it's Drinky Tree, Drinky Tree.

Squire: Ok, I'll try it once more. Drinky Tree, Drinky Tree, errrr. I've forgotten it now.

Nursie: **(She goes over to the Squire.)** You really are useless aren't you? All you say is "Drinky Tree, Drinky Tree, have you a nice little drink for me?"

(Nursie gets squirted from the tree. The Squire runs off laughing. Nursie chases off after him.)

For a change to the end, when the Squire says he has forgotten the words, he can ask the Audience to help him by shouting out the lines for him. When they all shout "Drinky Tree, Drinky Tree, have you a nice little drink for me?" The stage crew squirts the Audience with water pistols from the wings, or the tree can shoot out a small jet of water into the front few rows.

The Tree Of Truth

Another favourite routine. This has been presented in many pantomimes either with oranges, grapefruit, or coconuts. In Bob's version of *'The Pied Piper'*, it was called the 'Bush of Truth', and it didn't drop any fruit, but had stage crew behind the set with their arms through sleeve-like devices made to look like branches. These 'branches' would push the Dame and the Comic off the bench, or would take the Dames hat and throw it on the floor. (See Fig 9.) It is one of those routines that can be adapted in so many ways. We have also used this routine in our version of *'Treasure Island'*, to great comic effect by using coconuts.

(Enter Billy and Dame.)

Billy: I'm really tired, I've been busy all day sleeping. I must have a little sit down. **(He sits on bench under the tree.)**

Dame: Yes I'm tired as well. **(Sits next to Billy.)** I've been up since six o'clock this morning sweeping the floor and polishing the furniture.

(An orange falls on the Dame's head.)

Dame: Ow, what was that?

Billy: That was an orange. You are sitting under the tree of truth.

Dame: The tree of truth?

Billy: The tree of truth.

Dame: That's a daft name for a tree. What does it mean?

Billy: It means that every time you tell a fib an orange will fall from the tree and hit you on the head.

Dame: Well that won't bother me because I don't tell fibs.

(Another orange falls on the Dame's head.)

Billy: There you are, just as I said, an orange fell on your head - you must have told a lie.

Dame: **(All innocence.)** Moi, tell a lie?

Billy: Yes, you.

Dame: Well I didn't.

(Another orange falls on Dame's head.)

Billy: You must have told another one then.

Dame: It's a bit deaf. I've never done anything naughty in my life.

(Another orange falls on Dame's head.)

Billy: You're a bigger fibber than *[local town]* council.

Dame: I feel a bit chilly here. I think we should swap places. **(Gives Audience a little wink.)**

(Billy and Dame change places on the bench.)

Billy: Does that suit you now?

Dame: That's much better. Now tell me Billy, How much do you like me?

Billy: **(Flattering her.)** I think you're delightful.

(An orange falls on Billy's head.)

Dame: What was that?

Billy: Oh don't worry; I think it was just a loose one. The wind must have blown it down.

Dame: As I was saying. What do you really think of me?

Billy: Well, I think you're very...

(An orange on a line starts to descend slowly from the tree.)

Billy: ...different.

(The orange goes up.)

Dame: Yes, but do you think I look attractive?

Billy: Oh yes, you look very...

(Orange starts to descend.)

Billy: ...er ...I think that attractive is a very good word to use.

(Orange goes back.)

Dame: Do you know, I really think you're after me, aren't you? All these flattering compliments you keep giving me. Come on admit it, you're after my charms aren't you?

Billy: I didn't even know you had a charm bracelet.

Dame: Be honest, you are after me aren't you?

Billy: I... er... I think ... I...

(Orange starts to descend.)

Billy: Or maybe I'm ...

(Orange goes up.).

Dame: Well come along, it shouldn't take all night to give me an answer.

Billy: I'm overcome with emotion. The sight of your face has stunned me into silence. I can't answer - I'm so choked up.

Dame: Oh how touching. It's so nice to meet a man who is completely honest.

(A great big pile of oranges fall on top of them both.)

Fig 9 - *Colin Russell and Colin Pritchard performing the Bush of Truth from 'The Pied Piper' by Bob Heather.*

~~~(𝒟)~~~

The Uglies Boudoir Routine

There are many versions of the Uglies boudoir scene. Uglies is the term used in the theatre trade for the Ugly Sisters. It's a shame that there are very few pantomimes you can use this routine in with the exception of Cinderella. If you are creative enough, why not introduce similar sisters as your Comic Duo in a completely different pantomime script, but don't make them nasty – dare to be different. This is another of those routines that we wrote for a local theatre variety show. It is so easy to re-write and re-develop this routine - using all kinds of visual humour, from slapstick to slosh.

(On stage there is a dressing table Left, on which is a mirror, a mop-head powder puff, and some prop cosmetic pots. Set underneath it is a large packet of Pollyfilla, a bottle of Whiskey, a powerful water pistol, and a frying-pan containing a pancake. There is another dressing table Right, on which is a mirror, a mop-head powder puff and some prop cosmetic pots. Set underneath it is a powerful water pistol; a tin marked 'Gunpowder', and a Liquid Gumption spray bottle, or similar product. Make sure it is thoroughly clean. Asphyxia is sat at the Left table and Nausea at the Right, both in dressing gowns or onesies, and are discovered applying make-up)

Nausea: You know, Phixie dear, I think I'll give my face a nice mud-pack.

Asphyxia: I thought you already had, or did you fall in the ditch again on the way back from the *[local pub name]*?

Nausea: Well really sister dear.

Asphyxia: I'm not using a mud-pack anymore since that last lot of mud you got me came from a cow field - I think I'll try that new pancake make-up.

(Asphyxia takes out the frying-pan, flips up the pancake and slaps it onto her face.)

Asphyxia: How does it look?

Nausea: Much better. It hides your face beautifully. I've had some new powder given me. I was told it was just what I needed. **(She brings out the tin of gunpowder.)** It knocks spots off anything else I've tried.

Asphyxia: Yes, dear, I'm sure it that would remove your pimples nicely. **(She looks at Nausea then looks upwards and back to Nausea again with a puzzled expression.)** Is *that* what I saw embedded in the ceiling like buckshot last week?

Nausea: Well really – you're not perfect.

Asphyxia: Oh, but I am. **(She gives a little huf.)** Anyway I think I prefer my powder.

Nausea: Is it good?

Asphyxia: Very good, it makes my skin as smooth as a baby's bottom.

Nausea: Yes, and almost as dirty.

Asphyxia: Huh!

(Asphixia produces the Pollyfilla and starts powdering with her mop-head, raising large clouds of powder.)

Asphyxia: Now just a touch of perfume. **(She gets the Whiskey bottle; dabs some behind her ears, on her wrists, pours some down her bosom and looks to see if she's being watched before she takes a swig.)**

Nausea: I prefer my scent spray. **(She brings up the Liquid Gumption spray and sprays herself liberally with it.)** Oh Phixie dear, could you do the honours.

(Nausea hands Asphyxia the Liquid Gumption then bends right over. Asphyxia sprays Nausea's backside then hands the bottle back to her.)

Asphyxia: There you are sister dear - now we're ready to get dressed.

(Asphyxia and Nausea rise and take off their dressing-gowns or onesies, which they throw off Left and Right, displaying ludicrous underwear)

Asphyxia: Tighten my corset for me, dear. I want to look perfect for the Prince.

(Nausea gives a good hard tug at the strings and pulls Asphyxia over.)

Asphyxia: Careful Nausea.

Nausea: Well, hold on to something, then.

(Asphyxia holds on to Left side of pros arch and Nausea pulls. Asphyxia makes faces of excruciating agony)

Nausea: Can you still breathe?

Asphyxia: **(With breathing difficulty.)** I think so.

Nausea: Then it's not tight enough. **(She pulls harder)** Can you breathe now?

Asphyxia: No!

Nausea: That's all right then, I'll tie it off.

(Nausea pounces on Asphyxia knocking her over to tie them.)

Asphyxia: What a palaver! We'll never get to the ball tonight, at this rate. **(She gets up.)** We'd better get Buttons to help us into our dresses.

Nausea: Buttons? I wouldn't want to make him blush.

Asphyxia: Don't worry sister dear, everything is hidden under your wrinkles.

Nausea: Well really! If he's going to help us into our dresses, then I want him to do mine first.

Asphyxia: No, mine - I'm the eldest.

Nausea: Yes, it shows a mile.

Asphyxia: Don't you insult me like that. **(She slaps Nausea)**

Nausea: And don't you slap me. **(She slaps Asphyxia)**

Asphyxia: Well, don't you slap me, then. **(Hits Nausea with frying pan giving a lovely 'boyng' sound.)**

Nausea: Ow, that hurt. **(She reaches under her dressing table and takes out the water pistol and Squirts Asphyxia.)** Take that you minx.

(Asphyxia takes the water pistol from under her dressing table and starts squirting Nausea. They hear the Audience laughing, so both stop and turn to the Audience.)

Nausea: Who do you think you're laughing at?

Asphyxia: Come on sister; let 'em have it.

(Asphyxia and Nausea both start squirting the Audience.)

Just remember, there are so many things you can do with a boudoir routine, but don't fall into the trap of trying to put too much into it. Remember; always leave your Audience wanting more.

Fig 10 - *Heather Whitham performing the boudoir scene.*

~~~~(*D*)~~~~

The Red Hand Routine

This routine was created by Bob Heather for his version of *'Mother Goose'* that he wrote with Roger Lamb. It is a very simple routine yet ideal if you want a little more visual humour.

(A sign reads *"Madam Grisselda, Fortune Teller "*. Scrachit has been painting his cart and has a paint brush and paint tin. There is a little drop of liquid red make up in the tin.)

Bodjit: Don't go just yet. I'm waiting for someone.

Scrachit: Who are you waiting for?

Bodjit: I'm not telling you, you might think I'm daft.

Scrachit: It's all right, you can tell me, 'cause I think you're daft already.

Bodjit: Oh all right then. **(Pointing to sign.)** I'm waiting for the fortune teller to come.

Scrachit: Haven't you heard? - She won't be coming now, due to unforeseen circumstances

Bodjit: Oh. **(Holds out hand.)** I wanted my palm read

Scrachit: You wanted your palm read?

Bodjit: Yes. I wanted my palm read.

(Scratchit looks at Bodjit, then at the Audience and back to Bodjit again. He shakes his head then paints Bodjit's palm.)

Scrachit: There you are - one red palm.

Bodjit: Ugh, that's not fair.

(Sidney Snyde enters Down-Left.)

Snyde: **(To Bodjit.)** Caught you, you thief. You've been stealing my apples.

Scrachit: What makes you think they're yours?

Snyde: Of course they're mine - I'd recognise them anywhere. You've been to my orchard and stolen them. I caught you red 'anded **(Grabs Bodjit by right hand.)** Ugh

(Snyde lets go Bodjit's hand and looks at his own hand covered in paint. Make sure that Audience can see the paint.)

Bodjit: **(Laughing loudly.)** No, I've caught *you* red handed Squire.

Snyde: Why you...

(Snyde chases Bodjit and Scrachit off Left.)

Snyde: **(Shouting as he exits.)** Come back you rogues.

Fig 11 - *Bob Heather as Bodjit, and Andy Wolfe as Scrachit in 'Mother Goose' by Bob Heather and Roger Lamb.*

~~~(𝔇)~~~

The School-Room Routine

There are many versions of this routine used in pantomimes today. It is very easy to adapt, putting in all your favourite silly school jokes. There are lots of joke books available, but like all the other routines, don't put too much into your script. Less is often better than too much. This version of the School-room Routine is adapted from *'Babes in the Wood'* by Cheryl Barrett.

(The schoolroom has two benches Up-Left, and a trick bench in front. There is a blackboard and easel stage right, and a stool and desk for the teacher. On the desk there is a slapstick, blackboard rubber, and chalk. There is a chalk drawing of a beautiful woman on the blackboard with a small nail hammered in the blackboard just above her head – this nail shouldn't be seen by Audience. Holly, Daisy, and Poppy are already onstage playing around. Teddy and Tilly are seated on the middle bench. Much is seated on his own on the trick front bench. There is a general hubbub as Rosie enters ringing the bell.)

Rosie: Settle down, settle down.

(Holly, Daisy, and Poppy sit on the upstage bench behind Teddy and Tilly chatting loudly.)

Rosie: **(Shouts.)** Be quiet. **(Takes her mortar board off and puts it on her desk.)**

(Pupils quieten down.)

Rosie: That's better. Good morning, children.

All: Good morning, Miss.

Rosie: Who drew that picture on the blackboard?

Holly: **(Putting hand up.)** Please miss, it was Much.

Rosie: Was it you, Much?

Much: I didn't done it.

Rosie: **(Correcting him.)** I didn't *do* it.

Much: Well if I didn't done it and you didn't done it then who did done it?

Rosie: Whoever done…er, did it done a good job.

Daisy: Why's that, Miss.

Rosie: They've captured my beauty perfectly. Mind you the mystery artist forgot to put my mortar board on it.

(Much gets up walks to the blackboard, takes a piece of chalk and draws a hook on it around the nail. He takes the mortar board and hangs it on the hook above the picture.)

Rosie: What a clever boy you are. If I had any sweeties I would give you one.

Much: That's all right, Miss. You can have one of my toffees **(He takes a bag of sweets out of his pocket and offers the bag to Rosie.)** help yourself.

Rosie: **(Takes a toffee and pops it in her mouth.)** Thith ith really tasty and chewy.

Much: Yes, they were all covered in chocolate – but my dog licked all the chocolate off and spat the toffees out.

Rosie: **(Spitting the toffee in the bin.)** Why you naughty little… **(Grabs the slapstick from her desk.)** You'll get this if you don't behave. **(She brings the slapstick down hard on her hand and yells out in pain.)**

(The Pupils all laugh. Much grabs the bag of toffees and sits down on his bench.)

Holly: Please, Miss – who are the two new kids?

Rosie: What new kids? Where?

Teddy: Here, Nursie.

Tilly: Good morning, Nursie.

Rosie: Oh my, I'd forgotten all about you two. Class, please welcome Teddy and Tilly and make them feel at home.

Daisy: **(Takes a pair of slippers from her rucksack and gives them to Tilly.)** Put these on and I'll go and make you a cup of tea.

Rosie: **(To Daisy.)** What on earth are you doing?

Daisy: Making her feel at home. I always pop my favourite slippers on, have a cup of tea, and put my feet up as soon as I get home.

Rosie: Teddy - Tilly, I want you to ignore everything you are told.

Teddy: Absolutely everything?

Rosie: Absolutely. Now class, I want you to recite the alphabet.

(All the Pupils, with the exception of Teddy and Tilly recite the alphabet.)

All: A, B, C, D, E, F, G, H.

Rosie: **(Interrupting.)** Hold on a minute. Teddy, Tilly – why aren't you reciting the alphabet?

Much: They haven't found any letters they like yet.

Teddy: You told us to ignore everything we were told.

Rosie: I meant ignore what that rabble tell you. Do you understand why?

Tilly: Oh I see why.

Much: Tilly's found four letters she likes, Miss.

(The door swings open and Mean and Nasty rush in dressed as schoolboys.)

Rosie: Why are you late for my lesson?

Nasty: I thought it was our lesson.

Mean: We couldn't find the schoolroom.

Rosie: Couldn't find the schoolroom?

Much: Is there an echo in here?

Rosie: I left the door open for late comers.

Holly: Please Miss, Late Comers was expelled last week.

Nasty: Things keep changing.

Rosie: What sort of things?

Mean: Traffic lights.

Nasty: And the schoolroom door.

Mean: It looked like a door.

Nasty: But it was a jar.

Mean: That's why we're late.

Rosie: **(Indicates the downstage bench that Much is sitting on.)** Sit down over there and I'll deal with you two later.

(Mean and Nasty sit down on the downstage bench pushing Much closer to the Audience.)

Rosie: Right, I'll take the register. **(Looks on her desk.)** Where is it?

Poppy: Please Miss, Late Comers took it with him when he was expelled.

Rosie: You're all a bunch of rogues and lazy layabouts.

All: Thanks, Miss.

Rosie: I shall have to take the register the old way. Right – are you all here?

Much: We're all here, but we're not sure if you're all there.

Rosie: **(To Mean and Nasty.)** Now then, let's see what you two boys know. Without looking at the map on the wall, where are the Andes?

Much: **(Shakes his hands.)** At the end of his wristies.

Rosie: **(Looks over at Mean and Nasty.)** Right, who said that?

(Mean and Nasty stand up simultaneously and point at Much. The bench tips up and Much falls on the floor.)

Rosie: Come out here, Much.

(Much walks to the front of the class.)

Rosie: Hold out your handies.

(Rosie slaps Much's hand with the slapstick.)

Rosie: Now go and sit down.

Much: **(Walking back to his seat.)** S'not fair.

Rosie: Ok class - what is the name of the character who was turned into a donkey in A Midsummer Night's Dream?

Mean: Dobbin.

Nasty: Neddy.

Much: **(Calling out.)** Backside.

Rosie: **(Looks over at Mean and Nasty.)** Right, who shouted backside?

(Mean and Nasty stand up simultaneously and point at Much. The bench tips up and Much falls on the floor again.)

Rosie: Come out here, Much.

Much: (**Walking to the front of the class.**) I only shouted backside because I'm too polite to say Bottom.

Rosie: Let's hope you're not too polite to let me hit it.

(**Much bends over and Rosie slaps his backside with the slapstick.**)

Rosie: Now go and sit down.

Much: (**Walking back to his seat slowly rubbing his backside.**) I don't think I can sit. (**He sits.**)

Rosie: Right, now let's see what you all know about general knowledge. (**To Class.**) What's a Hindu?

Mean: } (**Together, standing up.**)
Nasty: } Lays eggs Miss.

(**As Mean and Nasty stand up, the bench tips and Much tumbles.**)

Rosie: Idiots, now sit down at once.

(**Much, Mean and Nasty all sit back on the bench.**)

Rosie: What is the outer part of a tree called?

All: (**Together.**) We don't know miss.

Rosie: Bark you imbeciles, bark.

All: (**Together, standing up and barking.**) Woof, woof, woof.

(**Much turns and winks at the Audience, then turns the bench round the opposite way and gives them a grin. While he is giving them the thumbs up, Mean and Nasty turn the bench back again to how it was.**)

Rosie: Quiet, the lot of you and sit down.

(**They all sit making sure Much is last to do so.**)

Rosie: I've had enough of you lot for today. (**She rings the bell.**) Time to go home.

(**They All jump up except Much, who goes flying to the floor once again as the bench tips. Black-out.**)

Here is another small piece that can be used in any school-room scene that you care to write. You can add several of the schoolroom jokes found at the back of this book if you wish, but don't overdo it.

Sarah: All right, let's see what you know. Um... **(She thinks for a couple of seconds.)** Ah yes, **(To Salt.)** Who defeated the Philistines?

Salt: I don't know. I don't follow American football.

Sarah: You are useless - what is a Hebrew?

Salt: A male tea bag.

Sarah: What's a baby hare called?

Pepper: A whisker miss.

Sarah: You are as bad as he is. Who knocked down to walls of Jericho?

Pepper: It wasn't me miss, I wasn't anywhere near it.

Salt: **(Standing up.)** If he said he didn't do it, he didn't do it - I was with him the whole time.

Fig 12 - *Dotty Latham, Lorraine Malloy and Bob Heather in the school-room scene from 'Mother Goose' by Norman Robins.*

For details on how to make a slapstick or construct a trick bench, see page 106.

Brain Food

This is a great little routine that can be used in almost any script even though we have given it the *'Aladdin'* flavour.

(Wishee is on stage talking to the Audience. Abanazar enters.)

Abanazar: There you are you fool?

Wishee: Yes, here I are. I say Uncle Abanazar - it's ever so good being rich now. My mum says she is wealthier than you now that Aladdin has the magic lamp.

Abanazar: Huh! That dratted boy.

Wishee: Oh Uncle, there is something I wanted to ask you – do rich people still have to go to school?

Abanazar: Of course they do, you won't learn everything unless you go to school. You'll never be brainy otherwise.

Wishee: Brainy?

Abanazar: Yes, brainy. You need to learn how to develop your brain.

Wishee: You seem to be a brainy chap yourself Uncle Abanazar – how do you develop brains?

Abanazar: Simple dear boy – simple. You need to eat lots of brain food such as fish.

Wishee: Fish?

Abanazar: Yes. It so happens that I have some wonderful fish all the way from Egypt, and I have bought it with me for my lunch.

Wishee: Really?

Abanazar: Oh yes. **(He takes a small foil wrapped package out of his pocket.)** Would you like it to develop your brains?

Wishee: Oh yes please.

Abanazar: Hang on a moment, it is very a special fish, and it's not cheap, but if you give me twenty gold coins, it's yours.

Wishee: Twenty gold coins? Ok Uncle I'll take it.

(**Wishee gives Abanazar twenty coins, and Abanazar gives Wishee the foil. Wishee opens it and takes out a slither of carrot** *[it looks like goldfish]*. **He holds it up.**)

Wishee: This looks good. (**He pops the carrot into his mouth.**) Mmmmm! That was really nice.

Abanazar: I'm so glad you enjoyed it my boy. Are you feeling any brainier?

Wishee: Oh yes, I think so. (**He realises.**) Hang on a minute Uncle, isn't twenty gold coins rather expensive for a little bit of fish like that?

Abanazar: It's working already – see how you're brains are developing. (**He exits laughing.**)

Wishee: I think I've been had. (**He chases off after Abanazar.**) Hey, come back with my money.

The Tyre Routine

This has always been an old favourite with professional pantomime comics adding the routine into whatever panto they happened to be in at the time. When we used it in our script '*Old King Cole*', it was changed from a tyre to a large gobstopper, to fit in with the fact that the routine was started by Candy Floss the Dame who owned the sweet emporium in the show.

If you decide to put it in the script for your society or drama company, then don't forget to change the names of the shops etc. to the ones in your area. If the script is intended for publication, then put in places for the performing company to add their localities in the direction notes.

(**Simon and Billy enter from opposite sides and meet. Simon has a car tyre in his hand.**)

Billy: What are you doing walking around with that tatty worn out old thing?

Simon:	Worn out and tatty. This tyre's not worn out and tatty.
Billy:	I wasn't talking to you – I was talking to the tyre.
Simon:	This is a magic tyre.
Billy:	A magic tyre? Tyres can't be magic. What does it do, roll down the road and turn into a side-street?
Simon:	No, no, no. This tyre is magic because it can go all the way around the town by itself.
Billy:	By itself? You mean without being fixed to a car?
Simon:	Without being fixed to a car and without a map.
Billy:	How does it find its way around this town without a map?
Simon:	Because it's magic, that's why.
Billy:	I'd like to see it do that.
Simon:	Would you like to see it do that?
Billy:	**(Looking behind him.)** Is there an echo in here?
Simon:	I'll tell you what I'll do - I shall make it go all the way around the town and come back here.
Billy:	This I have got to see. Come on, get it started.
Simon:	Watch closely.
Billy:	**(Moving to get a close look at the tyre.)** If I was watching any closer, I would get tyre marks on my face.

(Simon pushes the tyre off stage left and describes its journey around town using local street names. The following description of the tyre's journey must be spoken at a fast pace rather like a radio commentator describing a horse race. It is more effective if the journey described is a recognizable journey around the town the show is playing in.)

Simon:	There it goes - down the corridor, out of the stage door and into the street. It turns left at the end of the street into the High Street, down the High Street past Poundland, past the Dukes Head, now it's turning into East Street – past the Post Office and the greengrocers. It's now going down the hill and back into the High Street.

Billy: (Puts his hand to his ear.) I think I can hear it.

Simon: It's heading for the theatre. Oh, it nearly went past the stage door. It's ok, it's coming back and into the stage door, along the corridor and here it comes now.

(The tyre rolls on from stage right and is picked up by Billy.)

Billy: That was very good, but, it's strange you showing me a magic tyre – it's a co-inci-thingy.

Simon: Coincidence, idiot. Why is it strange?

Billy: It is strange because I happen to have a magic tyre as well. I'll go and get it.

(Billy walks to the side of the stage with the tyre. He holds the tyre off stage out of sight and talks to an unseen stage-hand.)

Billy: Will you take this tyre off me and hand me my magic tyre? Thank you kind sir. **(He immediately brings the same tyre back into view. He speaks to Audience, who obviously realize that it is the same tyre.)** Oh no it isn't.

Audience: Oh yes it is.

Billy: Oh no it isn't.

Audience: Oh yes it is.

Billy: It isn't. It just looks similar because it's the same colour.

Simon: Well come on then, set it off – I want to see this phenomena.

Billy: Do What? Right, here it goes. **(He rolls the tyre off stage left.)** There it goes down the corridor out of the stage door and it's stopped.

Simon: Why has it stopped?

Billy: It's thinking which is the quickest way to go.

Simon: Really?

Billy: It's off again along the High Street through the front door of Poundland, out the back door, round by McDonalds and it's stopped.

Simon: Why has it stopped by McDonalds?

Billy: It's eating some chicken nuggets.

Simon: Is it happy now?

Billy: Yes but the chicken's not very pleased. It's off again, through the park out the other side and it's stopped again.

Simon: Why has it stopped this time?

Billy: It's tired. It's off again - round the market place, through the park and it's stopped again.

Simon: Not again. What's it stopped this time for?

Billy: It's stopped for an ice-cream.

Simon: How can a car tyre eat an ice-cream?

Billy: It licks it.

Simon: It's going to be a very overweight tyre at this rate.

Billy: Don't worry; it's on a high fibre diet.

Simon: It'll be full of wind.

Billy: Well it saves you blowing it up. Here it comes now. Down the road, into the stage door, up the stairs into the circle, along the back of the circle, down the stairs, along the corridor, into the wings and here it comes now.

(Billy indicates stage left and a very large tractor inner tube is rolled on stage right and hits them in the back. As they both fall over there is a black-out.)

~~~~(*D*)~~~~

The Hat Routine

This routine can be used in most pantomimes, and almost anywhere within the script. It is a very simple routine and is ideal if you are looking for more visual humour. The director needs to rehearse this piece well to get the best from his cast in terms of reactions, comic timing, and the pace required for this routine.

(Dame, Billy, Ben and Jerry, all enter wearing hats. They stand in a line. The wicked Squire enters. The Audience boo.)

Squire: Oh shut it you lot or I'll make sure there are no ice creams in the interval.

(Audience reaction.)

Squire: Didn't you lot hear what I said?

Dame: Ooh, you rotten scoundrel.

Squire: Are you talking to me? Take your hat off when you speak to me.

Dame: I beg your puddin'?

Squire: **(He reaches out and takes Dame's hat off and throws it to the other end of the line-up.)** I said take your hat off when you speak to me.

(The Dame quickly whips Billy's hat and puts it on her own head. Billy then takes Ben's hat and puts it on his head. Ben does the same with Jerry's hat and puts it on. Jerry sees the Dames hat on the floor, picks it up, and puts it on.)

Dame: That's no way to treat a lady.

Squire: I told you to take your hat off when speaking to me. **(He reaches out and takes her hat off and throws it to the end of the line again.)**

(The Dame takes Billy's hat and puts it on, and so the whole thing repeats itself.)

This is best if it runs through four times until the Dame retrieves her own hat once again.

Knock Knock's, Jokes, and One-Liners

Knock knock jokes are great to use as running gags. You could sprinkle them through the whole show, spoken by anyone. Or you could write it in a way that just one character says them all the time. Another way of using them is to make one whole front-of-cloth scene with them. You have two characters talking about what has happened so far in the show, or enhancing the story, but they keep getting interrupted by several other members of the cast and chorus coming on stage interrupting with knock, knock jokes. (See also "Interruption Routines" on page 26)

It is entirely up to you how you use them in your script, but we always feel that a proper knock-knock joke should actually contain a real name, not just any old word being used as a name, it makes the joke funnier. Knock-knocks (as they are known in the pantomime trade) are very easy to think up and write, and can be used with Christian names of local dignitaries, or sports and entertainment stars, but here is a good selection for you to use freely in your scripts.

Knock, knock.
Who's there?
Justin.
Justin who?
Justin time to let me in.

Knock, knock.
Who's there?
Doctor.
Doctor who?

Knock, knock.
Who's there?
Ken.
Ken who?
Ken Billy come out to play?

Knock, knock.
Who's there?
Trish.
Trish who?
Bless you.

Knock, knock.
Who's there?
Felix.
Felix who?
Felix my lollipop again I'll bash him!

Knock, knock.
Who's there?
Dave.
Dave who?
Dave gone and locked the door again.

Now you have the idea, here is a list of names and conclusions.

Alan. door.	Alan nounce myself once you've opened the
Alex.	Alex the way you've done your hair.
Amos.	Amos quito is biting me - please let me in.
Andy.	Andy nother mosquito is biting me.
Anne.	Anne other mosquito is biting me.
Angus.	Angus me coat up and put the kettle on.
Anna. me out?	Anna nother thing – why do you keep locking

Annette.   Annette Curtain.

Annette.   Annette a whole pork pie.

Arnie.   Arnie ever going to open this door?

Bob.   **(Sings.)** Bob-in up and down like this.

Candy.   Candy owner of this horse and cart come and
     move it off my land.

Carla.   Carla taxi, I'm leaving.

Chester.   Chester minute – I think I'm in the wrong
     pantomime.

Chuck.   Chuck the key through the letter-box and I'll let
     myself in.

Colin.   Colin in for a chat.

Courtney.   Courtney door handle, can you open it and let me
     loose.

Courtney.   **(Sings.)** Courtney trap, can't go on. Oh how I
     love you so much baby…

Darren.   Darren other door I can use?

Donna.   Donna warm coat, it's chilly out here.

Fred.   Fred a needle, my coat's torn.

Isabel.   Isabel not working?

Ivan.   Ivan idea you're going to keep me waiting.

Jacqueline.   Jacqueline Hyde.

Jess.   Jess pass the key through the letter box and I'll open the door myself.

Joanna.   Joanna know who lives here?

Kim.   Kim yesterday but you weren't in.

Lily.   Lily pond.

Linda.   Linda hand to get this door open.

Luke.   Luke through the letterbox and you'll see who it is.

Matt.   Matt as well settle down, looks like I'm in for a long wait.

Mavis.   Mavis be the last time you keep me waiting.

Mike.   Mike your mind up

Mike.   **(Sings.)** Mike kind of town, Chicago is.

Omar.   Omar goodness, I've knocked on the wrong door.

Paul.   Paul the door open and you'll see who it is.

Paula.   Paula door from your side - it's a bit sticky.

Peggy.   Peggy washing up on the line, there's a bit of a breeze.

Penny.   Penny for your thoughts?

Phil. Phil this cup with sugar would you. I've run out.

Polly. Polly other one, it's got bells on.

Sarah. Sarah nother way in, or is this the only door?

Sam. **(Sings.)** Sam enchanted evening.

Seymour. Seymour of me by opening the door.

Sid. Sid you'd let me in ages ago.

Sid. Sid down and I'll explain.

Sid. **(Sings.)** Sid down you're rockin' the boat.

Will. Will I have to wait much longer?

Woody. Woody open the door if we asked him nicely?

Wendy. **(Sings.)** Wendy red, red robin comes bob, bob bobbin' along, along...

Wendy. Wendy you want me to call round again?

Wendy. Wendy you want us to stop these stupid knock, knock jokes?

This next assortment of jokes are ideal to sprinkle into your script in varying places, but don't get carried away. Always try to re-write the jokes or make them feel and sound different. Let's look at a few schoolroom jokes. In most pantomime schoolroom scenes, the Dame is generally the teacher.

(Child 1 enters. He/she is late for school.)

Dame: (To Child 1.) Where have you been?

Child 1: I've been throwing Peanuts in the river, miss.

Dame: Well you should have been here at Nine O'clock.

Child 1: Why – what happened miss?

Dame I'll deal with you later - go and sit down.

(Child 2 enters, also late.)

Dame: (To Child 2.) Another late-comer. Where have you been?

Child 2: I've been throwing Peanuts in the river miss.

Dame: Not you as well – go and sit down.

(Child 3 enters.)

Dame: Not another one? **(To Child 3.)** Don't tell me - I suppose you have also been throwing Peanuts in the river as well, haven't you?

Child 3: Oh no miss – I *am* Peanuts.

~~~~(𝒟)~~~~

Dame: Simon, go to the map and find America.

Simon: (Going up to the map and pointing.) Here it is!

Dame: Correct. Now, class, who discovered America?

Class: (Together, excitedly.) Simon did miss.

~~~~(𝒟)~~~~

Dame: Why are you late?

Billy: It's because of the sign down the road. It says, "School Ahead, Go Slow."

~~~~(𝒟)~~~~

Dame: Billy, you are wearing odd socks.

Billy: I've got another pair at home exactly the same.

~~~~(𝒟)~~~~

Dame: Billy, why are you doing your sums on the floor?

Billy: You told me to do it without using tables!

~~~~(𝕯)~~~~

Dame: Yesterday I gave you all a picture of a duck holding an umbrella and told you all to colour the duck yellow and the umbrella green, however, Billy coloured the duck in bright red.

Billy: Yeah, good isn't it?

Dame: How many times have you ever seen a red duck?

Billy: The same number of times I've seen a duck holding an umbrella, Miss.

~~~~(𝕯)~~~~

Dame: Now then Billy – if I gave you a penny, Simon gave you a penny, and Jane gave you a penny, how much would you have?

Billy: Nothing miss.

Dame: How do you work that out?

Billy: Because I would have bought a strawberry ice cream with it.

~~~~(𝕯)~~~~

Dame: Billy, can you tell me what the four seasons are?

Billy: Salt, pepper, mustard, and vinegar.

~~~~(𝕯)~~~~

Dame: What do you call a person who keeps on talking when people are no longer interested?

Jack: A teacher.

~~~~(𝕯)~~~~

Dame: Billy, give me a sentence starting with "I".

Billy: I is the...

Dame: **(Interrupting.)** No, Billy. Always say, "I am."

Billy: All right... I am the ninth letter of the alphabet.

~~~(𝔇)~~~

Dame: Simon, you've failed the maths test so many times I've lost count.

Simon: Now you know how I feel, miss.

~~~(𝔇)~~~

Dame: Simon, your homework on "My Dog" is exactly the same as your brother's. Did you copy it?

Simon: No, miss, it's the same dog!

~~~(𝔇)~~~

Dame: How can you prevent diseases caused by biting insects?

Billy: Please miss - don't bite any.

~~~(𝔇)~~~

Dame: What is the centre of gravity?

Jack: The letter "V"

~~~(𝔇)~~~

(Jack is the Dame's favourite pupil.)

Dame: Jack, name two pronouns.

Jack: Who, me?

Dame: Very good – well done my boy.

~~~(𝔇)~~~

Billy: Please Miss, what would happen if I took the school bus home?

Dame: The police would make you bring it back, you stupid boy!

~~~(𝒟)~~~

Dame: To which family does the elephant belong?

Jack: I don't know no-one that owns one in our street.

~~~(𝒟)~~~

Dame: Can you think of a solution to end unemployment?

Jack: Yes, Miss. I'd put all the men on one island and the women on another.

Dame: And how will that work?

Jack: They would all be busy building boats.

~~~(𝒟)~~~

Teacher: Where is your homework?

Jack: I lost it fighting the school bully. He said you were the worst teacher in the school.

~~~(𝒟)~~~

Jack: Please Miss, I ain't got no crayons.

Dame: Young man, you mean, I don't have any crayons. **(Then explaining to the Class.)** You don't have any crayons. We don't have any crayons. They don't have any crayons. Do you see what I'm getting at?

Jack: Yes miss - what happened to all the crayons?

~~~(𝒟)~~~

Simon:	Miss, Wally took a ruler to bed last night.
Dame:	Why did you do that, Wally?
Wally:	Because I wanted to see how long I slept!

~~~~($\mathcal{D}$)~~~~

Dame:	You boy, what's your name?
Mickey:	Mickey Mongoose.
Dame:	We'll just call you Mongoose when calling the register - we don't use first names.
Mickey:	My dad will be furious – he doesn't like it when people take the Mickey out of my name.

~~~~($\mathcal{D}$)~~~~

Dame:	What did your mother do yesterday morning, Simon?
Simon:	She done her shoppin' at the Co-op, Miss.
Dame:	Done her shoppin at the Co-op', Simon? Where's your grammar?
Simon:	She's doin' her shoppin' at the Co-op too, Miss.

~~~~($\mathcal{D}$)~~~~

Dame:	What's the longest piece of furniture in school?
Billy:	The multiplication table.

~~~~($\mathcal{D}$)~~~~

Now for a few jokes involving the Dame, with or without other characters being involved.

Dame:	**(To Comic.)** Look at me when I'm lying to you

~~~~($\mathcal{D}$)~~~~

Dame: I just bought 35 cans of women's deodorant - I can't help it, I'm an impulse buyer

~~~~(𝒟)~~~~

Dame: I never wanted to believe that my late husband was stealing from his job as a road worker, but when I got home all the signs were there.

~~~~(𝒟)~~~~

Comic: She's got a face that could make an onion cry

~~~~(𝒟)~~~~

Dame: Do you know what I like about you?
Squire: No, what?
Dame: Nothing

~~~~(𝒟)~~~~

Dame: **(During her intro chat to Audience.)** Do you like the frock? Peacock's special – buy one, get one free. This is the free one

~~~~(𝒟)~~~~

Dame: I've got no change.
Landlord: That's no change.

~~~~(𝒟)~~~~

Comic: **(He gives the Dame a pheasant.)** Your game.
Dame: Shhh, don't tell everyone.

~~~~(𝒟)~~~~

Dame: (She enters with a handful of envelopes.) Oh look at this lot. Everyone wants money from me.
Comic: Are those all bills?
Dame: No they're all mine.

~~~(𝔇)~~~

Dame: Are you a man or mouse?
Comic: I must be a man because you're afraid of mice.

~~~(𝔇)~~~

Dame: I'm off home; I've got work to do.
Billy: Like what?
Dame: I'm going to windows then I have to surf the net.
Billy: I didn't know you had a computer.
Dame: Who said anything about a computer - when I said going to windows and surf the net, I mean I'm going to wash the curtains.

~~~(𝔇)~~~

Dame: I have a vested interest at heart.
Squire: You have a heart?

~~~(𝔇)~~~

Dame: I went to the bank yesterday to ask the manager if he could check my balance, so he pushed me over.

~~~(𝔇)~~~

Dame: I was going to put some toilet water behind my ears, but the seat keeps falling down and clobbering me.

~~~(𝔇)~~~

Dame: I phoned up and asked the man from *[local]* council if I could have a skip outside my house. He said I could skip where I liked as long as I didn't make any noise.

~~~(𝕯)~~~

Comic: (**To Dame.**) You are a softy really, do you cry at weddings?

Dame: Only my own.

~~~(𝕯)~~~

Billy: What lies at the bottom of the sea and shivers?

Simon: I dunno.

Billy: A nervous wreck.

~~~(𝕯)~~~

Dame: When I was at the market, I bought four sizes of Bra. Egg cup, D cup, world cup, and my cup runneth over.

~~~(𝕯)~~~

Dame: The kitchen is so small; we can only use condensed milk.

~~~(𝕯)~~~

Dame: (**Saying her hello's to Audience.**) Oh look at this. Is Agnes Green in tonight? (**Looks around Audience.**) Where is she? Agnes is one hundred and eleven today. **(A child from Junior Chorus runs on and whispers in Dame's ear, then runs off again.)**

Dame: Oh sorry. Agnes isn't a hundred and eleven, she's ill.

~~~(𝕯)~~~

Squire: I haven't seen you for some time. My how you've changed.

Dame: Yes, I've put on a teensy-weensy little bit of weight in the interim.

Squire: Yes, and you've put quite a lot on in the outer-rim as well.

Dame: Will you still love me when I'm old and wrinkled?

Comic: Let's not talk about tomorrow, shall we?

Dame: Every day it's the same - take this week. On Monday I got toothache, on Tuesday I got headache, on Wednesday I got stomach ache, Thursday I got backache, Friday I got fruke ache.....

Comic: Fruke ache?

Dame: Yes from my sister in *[nearby local town]*. She makes wonderful fruitcakes.

Now here are a few jokes that you can give to almost anyone.

Duo 2:   My mum's a black belt in k-k-k

Duo 1:   Karate?

Duo 2:   No. In ki-ki-ki

Duo 1:   Oh, in kick boxing?

Duo 2:   No the kitchen.

Duo 1:   In the kitchen?

Duo 2:   Yes. One of her chops, and you're dead.

Griselda: **(She is reading a note from the Wicked Stepmother.)** She says "Please be home before I am".

Gertrude: How are we supposed to know when she gets home? Let's have a look at that. **(She snatches note.)** You idiot. It says "Please be home before one a-m".

~~~~(𝒟)~~~~

Dame: Oh, I'm ever so lonely. Do you know what? I went to one of those lonely hearts club meetings the other day and all the men said the same thing to me - "I'm not *that* lonely".

~~~~(𝒟)~~~~

Simon: I used to wonder where the sun went, so I stayed up all night to see where it had gone – then it dawned on me.

~~~~(𝒟)~~~~

Simon: How do you make Lady Gaga unhappy?
Billy: I don't know.
Simon: Poker-face.

~~~~(𝒟)~~~~

Comic: I was wondering why the horse and cart kept getting bigger and bigger – then it suddenly hit me.

~~~~(𝒟)~~~~

Billy: I've lost my little doggie and can't find him anywhere.
Jack: Have you tried putting an ad in *[local paper]*?
Billy: Don't be daft. He can't read.

~~~~(𝒟)~~~~

Duo 2:	I just saw a monkey with a tin opener.
Duo 1:	Really?
Duo 2:	I said, "You don't need a tin opener to peel a banana".
Duo 1:	What did he say?
Duo 2:	He said, "No, this is for the custard".

~~~~(𝒟)~~~~

Comic: (**Introducing.**) Ladies and gentlemen, boys and girls. Tonight we have five minutes of entertainment crammed into two hours of pure chaos.

~~~~(𝒟)~~~~

Billy:	I bought four suits for a pound.
Simon:	How can you buy four suits for a pound?
Billy:	I bought a pack of playing cards.

~~~~(𝒟)~~~~

In a chase scene, the Comic Duo can get off the stage and run round the auditorium. When they get back to the stage, the Dame or Comic can say - "This time you've gone too far." They reply, - "No, we only went up there, along there, and down there." Pointing out their route.

~~~~(𝒟)~~~~

An idea for a Dame's outfit - a pretty girl is embroidered on the underskirt, so that when the dame enters, she holds the front of the skirt above her head, and dances on, looking like a can-can dancer. She then drops the skirt to reveal that it is indeed her prancing her way on stage.

~~~~(𝒟)~~~~

HOW TO MAKE A SLAPSTICK

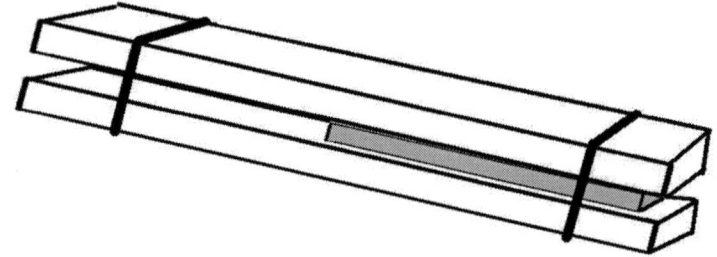

Fig 13 – *How to make a slapstick.*

The slapstick is made from two school rulers held together at each end by a rubber band. There is a small sandwich of foam-rubber inserted into one end. The user holds the slapstick by the end containing the foam-rubber. It will make a healthy and audible slap when struck on anything or anyone. You do not have to slap hard in order for a good sound. The above illustration is not to scale.

HOW TO CONSTRUCT A TRICK SCHOOL-ROOM BENCH

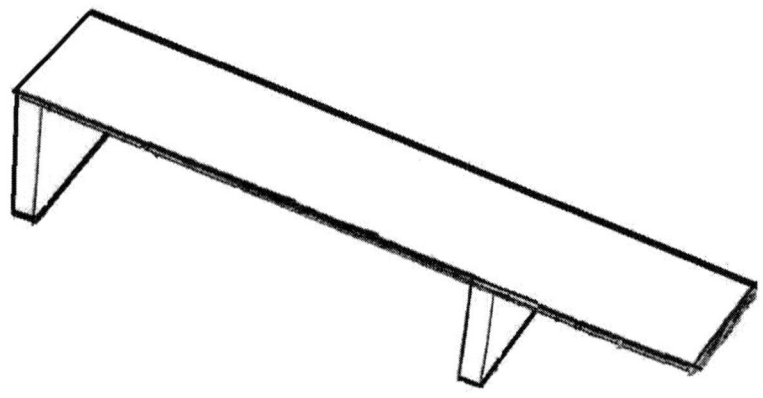

Fig 14 – *Trick bench construction.*

The trick bench is easily constructed by making the top for a normal bench. When positioning the legs, place one of the sets of legs in the normal position for a bench, and the other set should be inboard by a third of the bench length as shown in the diagram above. Note – the character that is supposed to fall off whenever the others get up, should sit on the overhanging end of the bench. This needs extra rehearsal time as timing is critical so that the fall-guy is aware of when the others will let him fall. When the fall-guy lands, it can add to the humour if he can perform a comical landing such as going head over heels, or falls off the stage. (Assuming the stage is not too high.) The above illustration is not to scale.

Fig 15 – *Authors Bob Heather and Cheryl Barrett with Sir Ian McKellen at one of their pantomime workshops.*

PANTOMIME SKILLS
WORKSHOP
FOR DIRECTORS AND ACTORS

**Your group will benefit from
Cheryl Barrett and Bob Heather's
vast pantomime experience**

At the all-day workshop (5hrs), we will cover:-

Pantomime traditions
How to inject visual comedy into your show
Ensure your pantomimes are slick, polished, and full of pace
Traditional routines and "business"
Comic Duo's, Dames and other comic characters
Baddies and Goodies – boo and hiss
Interacting with chorus and audience

We will be working from prepared scripts - this is a practical
workshop and participants should wear appropriate clothing

www.dublar.co.uk/pantoworkshops.html

workshops@dublar.co.uk